Universities

The Recovery of an Idea

Universities

The Recovery of an Idea

Gordon Graham

IMPRINT ACADEMIC

Copyright © Gordon Graham, 2002

The moral rights of the author have been asserted
No part of any contribution may be reproduced in any form
without permission, except for the quotation of brief passages
in criticism and discussion.

Published in the UK by Imprint Academic
PO Box 1, Thorverton EX5 5YX, UK

Published in the USA by Imprint Academic
Philosophy Documentation Center
PO Box 7147, Charlottesville, VA 22906-7147, USA

ISBN 0 907845 37 1

A CIP catalogue record for this book is available from the
British Library and US Library of Congress

Contents

Preface

The first version of this book was written almost five years ago, but was unable to find a publisher. I approached no fewer than eleven and all of them said that academic interest is now so specialized, no one would be interested in reading what is essentially an academic book about universities in general. In the belief, or at least the hope, that this could not be so, I produced copies for distribution to people I thought might be interested. It was picked up and included in the Booknotes section of the journal *Philosophy*, and as a result I had quite a number of requests for copies, a number sufficient to suggest that the publishers were wrong about the level of interest. I would like to record my thanks to all those who wrote to me appreciatively about my attempt to prompt a debate about modern British universities that would avoid partisanship and employ the same sort of standards that the best academic inquiry prides itself on.

Eventually, by good fortune I encountered an interested publisher. This gave me the opportunity to revise the text, to note the appearance in the meantime of *The New Idea of a University* by Duke Maskell and Ian Robinson, and to update the sections on teaching quality, research assessment and student fees. I am very grateful to Keith Sutherland of Imprint Academic for being willing to take chances other publishers will not take, and to Dr Robert Grant of Glasgow University for pointing me in his direction.

Gordon Graham
King's College
University of Aberdeen
April 2002

Introduction

The title of this book has been chosen in allusion to John Henry Newman's *The Idea of a University*. Newman's essay was originally a series of lectures (or 'Discourses') delivered in Dublin in advance of the establishment of the Catholic University of Ireland in 1854. The essay first appeared as a set of pamphlets, soon after to be bound together and is still in print.

The context for these lectures was a dispute which has no interest for most people today. Newman was providing a theoretical defence of the Irish Catholic hierarchy's objection to the secular university colleges established in Ireland by the British Government in 1845 (though ironically this Catholic alternative eventually formed the basis of the National University of Ireland which united most of these same colleges). He mounts his defence on the strength of a thesis that is unlikely to meet with much support in contemporary universities, namely the impossibility of a secular, non-religious university education. As a consequence of this context, a central part of his argument has to do with the role and teaching of theology, a subject absent from the curricula of most modern British universities, and a minority subject where it is still taught. A further, substantial part of the lectures is devoted to reconciling the authority of the church with the investigations of modern science, another topic likely to be of limited interest today. Yet despite these important differences between Newman's time and ours, *The Idea of a University* (especially Discourses V, VI and VII) still has things to say that are relevant to thinking about contemporary universities.

More surprising than this continuing relevance, however, is the fact that in the century and a half since Newman wrote, his book has had no significant successor, even though monumental changes have taken place in universities during this same period. Indeed, more striking still is the fact that Newman's is one of very few attempts *ever* made to think directly about the nature and purpose of a university. Given the age of the institution, and its importance to the intellectual and cultural life of this country over many centuries, this is a remarkable fact.

There is one recent exception to this generalization, namely *The New Idea of a University* by Duke Maskell and Ian Robinson (London, 2001) which expressly discusses Newman, and deplores what it sees as a radical departure among contemporary universities from the 'old' idea. According to Maskell and Robinson in recent times "[t]he university has been remade not in defiance of Newman but in indifference to him. But he says things that, if anybody paid attention to them, could not fail to kill instantly our new orthodoxy about the universities making us rich" (Maskell and Robinson 2001: 25). Now, whatever the justice of their complaint, the fact is as I have just suggested — the context of Newman's lectures was inevitably quite different to that of the present day. His *Discourses* undertake to characterize and defend what has come to be known as a liberal education. Though often cited in defence of more arcane subjects by university teachers, the actual influence that is to be attributed to his book has probably been overestimated. It is the traditional American liberal arts college that has come closest to Newman's ideal, not the universities of Britain from whose experience his reflections arose. There is to my mind a dangerous romanticism in thinking that once upon a time British universities were suitably Newmanesque until the arrival of utilitarian Philistines, and Maskell and Robinson constantly run the risk of falling into this trap. In several places Newman's 'arguments' are weak, as it seems to me, and to call upon them is unlikely "to kill instantly" the ideas that have won favour in the minds of many modern academics. Nevertheless there is something important to emulate in Newman's enterprise — the spirit of inquiring clearly and critically into the very idea of a university and its value.

The purpose of this book, then, is not to review or revitalize Newman's arguments, though, since a number of the themes he addresses are still topical, I shall refer to some of his claims from time to time in the chapters that follow. Nor is it my aim to deplore the present and lament the past, a charge that might not wholly inaccurately be brought against Maskell and Robinson. Rather, my purpose in writing is to draw attention to a number of interrelated issues that are of considerable contemporary significance, to examine them in a sustained way and, it is to be hoped, begin a discussion that is long overdue — namely some inquiry into how we should regard universities and what it is reasonable to expect from them.

Such a discussion (as I shall conduct it) is an exercise in two branches of philosophy — philosophy of education and applied philosophy. Interestingly, the recent history of both is singularly different. The philosophy of education, after a short lively period dominated by R.S. Peters, is in the doldrums. Even at its height, the philosophy of higher education never got much attention. By contrast, applied philosophy, the attempt to relate philosophical questions to social and moral issues, has flourished in recent years as never before. It has largely been concerned with ethical questions and with public issues related, in one way or another, to the question of social justice. Yet there is good reason to think, as I hope to show, that the traditional questions of philosophy of education, which have to do with learning, understanding, science, practical training and the value of knowledge, have important implications in the sphere of social policy with respect to higher education.

The task of exploring these implications is difficult for two reasons. Any discussion of the nature and conduct of universities at the present time runs the risk of being pigeon-holed, that is, of being automatically bracketed with one of two opposed positions. On the one side there is the modernizer who believes that old ideas must be abandoned in the face of the necessity to deal with 'reality', and on the other there is the 'traditionalist' who believes that every such move sells the pass on values and institutions that are vital to civilization as we know it, and to which we should fight to return. *The New Idea of a University* might plausibly be said by its critics to fall into the latter camp.

Yet these two views are caricatures of each other, and if serious thinking about universities and the policies which should govern them is to take place, it is essential that the straight-jacketed thinking this sort of dichotomy inevitably induces be abandoned. Both contemporary conditions and educational history are more complex than would favour either position — and hence the sort of thinking that needs to be done must be more complex too. This very complexity, however, gives rise to the second difficulty. The variety of topics that need to be considered if we are to introduce any measure of coherence into thinking about the modern university is very considerable. It is necessary to sketch the history of the institution, to consider the ideas of higher education and academic research, to record recent social trends, to look at a spectrum of social policies, to explore cultural images, to examine educational methods, and to review the economics of public finance. This range of tasks is somewhat daunting. Yet it is at heart, in my view, philosophical, and it is questions in the philosophy of education which must make the running.

Such is the scope of these questions, however, that it is not possible to offer the last word on any of the topics under review. On the other hand, there is something to be said for sticking one's head above the parapet and offering the first word. I am firmly convinced that though the topics with which this book deals are philosophical, they are also of public importance, and I have attempted to relate the relatively abstruse to the relatively practical. This is the mark of 'applied' philosophy. I also think that they have not been addressed in a sustained or measured way, and that doing so might contribute something towards ameliorating the confusion and, indeed, malaise, by which life in contemporary British universities is marred. At any rate this is something reasonable to attempt.

Philosophy at its best is marked by clarity and rigour. There are topics that are not properly speaking those of philosophy, yet there are things about them that only a philosopher would, or could, say. The nature of a university is one of these. I hope that my professional mode of analytical thinking and writing has enabled me to preserve philosophy's intellectual virtues in the exploration of the many issues which I believe need to be addressed. If I have, the book will have the merit of setting out certain questions, and some answers to them, in a manner which makes their debate more precise, and hence more profitable. At any rate this is my aim and, given the breadth of the subject, to have realised it is as much as could be reasonably wished for.

CHAPTER 1

A Very Short History of British Universities

The Mediaeval University

No one can say precisely when university education began in Britain. Although we know that Oxford was Britain's first university, and was founded after Paris, Bologna and several others on the continent of Europe, we do not know exactly when 'the clerks of Oxenford' first started to study and teach. The early part of the twelfth century seems likely, perhaps because from 1167 English students were barred from attending the University of Paris. Certainly, by the end of the twelfth century, Oxford was established to a degree sufficient for it to be regarded as a distinct place of learning. Then in 1207, or thereabouts, some of the Oxford clerks migrated to Cambridge, and England's second university began. Amazingly enough, it was over six hundred years before a third was founded, The two universities added very many constituent colleges over this long period, of course, but while in these colleges fellows taught and students learned, it was the universities that had the right to confer degrees. And of these, for the greater part of English educational history, there were only two.

But the third university in the British Isles came into existence not so very long after, at St Andrews in Scotland. Started somewhere between 1411 and 1413, permission to found Scotland's first university was given initially by the renegade Pope in Avignon, though readily confirmed by Rome when the schism which had resulted in the existence of two rival popes ended. In the course of the same cen-

tury further universities were established at Glasgow (1451) and
Aberdeen (1495) also by the express authority of the Pope. Both
drew their inspiration from Europe, the first Principal of Aberdeen
coming from the University of Paris. In 1583 the University of Edinburgh was founded. Edinburgh was different to all the rest, both
North and South of the border, in that, though it was inspired by
Presbyterianism, it was a civic rather than a religious foundation
(and to this day has no college chapel). It was the City Fathers, not
the Church Fathers who called it into existence and the Crown which
gave it the authority to confer degrees. But before the end of the century there was one further religious foundation in Scotland. The Ref-
ormation brought about the establishment in Aberdeen in 1593 of a
Protestant rival to King's College, named Marischal College after the
Protestant Earl Marischal of Scotland who was its creator, and for
over two hundred and fifty years (until 1860) they remained separate universities, allowing Aberdonians to boast that their city had
as many universities as the whole of England.

A little earlier (1591) Dublin University, with just one college
(Trinity) had come into existence, modeled closely on the Oxbridge
pattern. As Ireland's first and oldest university, it became a place of
some distinction in its own right, being the *alma mater* of Oliver
Goldsmith and Edmund Burke amongst others, though it never
quite emerged from the shadow of Oxford. The fact that for the first
three hundred years of its existence only Anglicans were allowed to
attend it, gave it the image and reputation of both a representative
and a bastion of the Protestant Ascendancy, which it retained until
well after the Republic of Ireland had been established. As a consequence, though it was Ireland's only university for 250 years, until
very recently it was never really an Irish one.

By the end of the sixteenth century, then, Britain had eight universities, five in Scotland, two in England, one in Ireland. It was over a
hundred years before there were any more. With the exception of
Edinburgh, they were all religious foundations, of greatly differing
sizes. As in their continental counterparts, their founding subjects
were Theology, Law and Arts and a large part of their purpose was
to provide education originally designed for the professional classes
of the middle ages. This was less true of Edinburgh and Dublin, and
in all of them other interests and subjects developed of course, medicine having been on the curriculum since early times in Scotland. But
up to this point British universities were inheritors of, and for the
most part formed by, the mediaeval conception of a university.

When the next wave of universities came, they arose from a rather different spirit and took a different form.

The Modern University

In this respect, however, in comparison with other European countries Britain was slow to develop the modern university, if we characterise the modern university as a non-denominational institution in which natural science played a significant part and where theology and history were subject to critical intellectual scrutiny. This was less true in Scotland. There, university professors such Francis Hutcheson and Adam Smith played an important part in the Scottish Enlightenment, and the University of Edinburgh established itself at the forefront of medical science. But it was Germany that led the way in the transformation of the mediaeval university, the first stirrings of this new conception usually being associated with the establishment of the University of Halle, by Lutherans, as early as 1694. And it was in Germany too that it developed most rapidly, so that by 1809 the University of Berlin was offering laboratory based courses in experimental sciences, a sharp contrast with the educational goals still being pursued in Oxford, which, according to Newman "after a century of inactivity . . . was giving no education at all to the youth committed to its keeping".

It was another twenty years, and 133 years after the foundation of Halle, before Britain showed signs of following suite. London University (later University College London), opened its doors in 1827, called into being by the desire to provide mechanics and other relatively lowly occupations with education, quite irrespective of religion. Because it admitted Jews, Roman Catholics and Non-conformists, London University was denied a charter, and so was unable to award degrees. But its creation still had its effect. Within four years it prompted the establishment in London of another new university college – King's – which, being an Anglican foundation, was able to obtain a charter. (In 1843 King's London was replicated in the Queen's College, Birmingham. Queen's also received a royal charter, but ironically its was being an Anglican foundation in the strongly non-conformist Midlands which, in the end, prevented it from becoming a fully fledged university). In 1836, King's was followed by the creation of the University of London, organized on a federal pattern. Over the next few decades other colleges opened, existing colleges became affiliated, and the result was that England finally had in its capital city a third, large university, one with a quite different character to the two ancient universities which had existed for so long before.

A notable feature of the new university was the provision in 1849 for 'external' as well as 'internal' students, that is to say, students who could study for London degrees at home and at a distance, rather than being required to be resident in a constituent college. The creation and relatively rapid growth of London University had several important effects. First, the much looser federal structure than had existed in Oxford and Cambridge was quickly copied in other parts of the British Isles. The 1840's saw the creation of university colleges in Belfast, Dublin, Cork and Galway, later united into the National University of Ireland. Not long after, the University of Wales began, also a federal structure. Second, the fact that it was possible to study for a degree at London university while continuing to live elsewhere broke the traditional residential pattern of the ancient universities of England and thus extended higher education to a far wider section of the population. This was a more notable change in England than in Scotland. Existing as they did in what was generally a poorer country, the Scottish universities did not attract large endowments, and tended to serve a much less affluent class of student. Nor were they confined by the same religious restrictions. Indeed, for quite a time, the only access poor students from England and Ireland had to higher education was by attending Scottish universities where it was possible to pay relatively small fees for tuition and examination and make one's own arrangements for board and lodging.

The 'external' examination system developed in London also made it possible for people in relatively far flung parts of the empire to take degrees, and thus it was that the London pattern and character of university education came to be a major influence on the development of higher education in other parts of the world. Its influence was not exclusive, however. The Scottish tradition, with an emphasis on broadly based, rather than highly specialised degree courses, was very influential in Canada and Australasia.

At the time that London was founded, the emergence of new universities seems, somehow, to have been in the air, perhaps because the British became aware of an unflattering contrast with continental Europe. It is sometimes disputed whether the claim of being England's third university does not belong to Durham rather than London, because there was an abortive attempt to establish a university there in the 1650's during the period of Cromwell. But it was not until much later — 1832 — that a further attempt was successful. In any case, though Durham eventually spawned the University of Newcastle, it was the existence of London University which was chiefly responsible for the next phase of university expansion in Britain. Colleges that initially prepared students for London degrees fairly quickly became universities in their own right. This was true in several major cities, notably, Bristol, Birmingham and Manchester, the Victoria University College in Manchester being founded in 1851, Mason's College Birmingham in 1875 and University College Bristol in 1876. Several of these in turn gave birth to other colleges which then became autonomous — Liverpool and Hull are instances — all of them coming to be known collectively as the 'red brick' universities.

Given the federal structure of London and Wales and the creation of the Irish Free State which removed most of the National University of Ireland colleges from the British system (Queen's, Belfast was the exception), the precise number of universities in Britain by 1950 is not in itself altogether significant for purposes of comparison. But whatever way they are counted, the preceding hundred years had witnessed a dramatic expansion of institutions, academics, subjects and students, with a very much wider spectrum of people having access to higher education, greatly enhanced by the admission of women from the 1880's onwards. Even so, the participation rate was still relatively small, not much more than two or three percent of the school population probably, though higher in Scotland than in the rest of the United Kingdom. It was notably lower than in several European countries, and dramatically less than in the United States or Canada. It was concern about this poor participation rate that led to the next expansive phase, a consequence of deliberate Government policy.

The Robbins Report of 1960 recommended the creation of a large number of wholly new universities. The motivation behind it was partly economic and partly egalitarian — to provide Britain with a population sufficiently highly educated to capitalise upon rapidly changing economic and technological conditions, and to ensure that anyone who had the ability to benefit from tertiary education could do so irrespective of their financial circumstances. The result was the formation over the next few years of the so-called 'plate glass' universities. These had several distinguishing features. First, they were purpose built on green field 'campus' sites. Second, it was not just the buildings that were planned '*de novo*'. Most of the new institutions made special attempts to depart from traditional forms of degree course and academic organization. Thus the University of Stirling adopted a continental two 'semester' system rather than the normal pattern of three terms, the Universities of Sussex and East Anglia taught in interdisciplinary 'schools' rather than the customary 'departments', and several others founded new and interdisciplinary degrees in, for example, American Studies or Comparative Literature.

Polytechnics

Dramatic though these developments in universities were, they do not tell the whole story of the expansion of higher education in Britain. The nineteenth century faith in self-improvement, and education as a means to it, had thrown up very many 'mechanics institutes' whose purpose was to provide the artisan classes with the means of acquiring more directly 'useful' skills than were available in the traditional university, or even in the new universities of London and Durham. It was not long, however, before many of these began to interest themselves in the more theoretical sides of 'the mechanical arts', and subjects such as engineering and pharmacology made an appearance in their curriculum. Some of these became universities after a time — the Universities of Strathclyde and Loughborough are notable examples, as is the Royal Technological Institute in Manchester which became the University of Salford. That is to say, they became autonomous institutions entitled to set their own standards and award their own degrees. But others became Colleges of Technology, governed, like schools, by local authorities and subject, also like schools, to external scrutiny.

In the later 1960's it became government policy to expand this sector of education also. And so the polytechnics came into existence, though the name was not adopted in Scotland where they continued to be known as Colleges of Technology. As inheritors of the mantle of the old mechanics' institutes, the principal purpose of the polytechnics was to provide a practical, technological education. However, before long, the range of subjects taught in polytechnics expanded to include social studies and some of the arts and humanities. Degree courses in all these disciplines were subject to the scrutiny and approval of the Council for National Academic Awards, and the polytechnics remained under the financial control of local authorities. It was inevitable, as the range of subjects grew, that 'the Polys' would come to regard with envy the academic autonomy and relative financial independence of the universities. A factor, too, was their status. By and large, universities were regarded, by those within and without them, as having a 'superior' educational status, and this comparison was exacerbated as the Polys offered more subjects which had been the traditional prerogative of the universities.

All this was altered by the education reform acts of 1988 and 1992. Among other important changes, together these granted polytechnics degree awarding autonomy, and financial independence from local authorities. The 1992 act also allowed them to apply for university status, and in the first few years of the 1990's almost all of them of them were granted it, virtually doubling the number of universities in Britain, roughly from fifty to a hundred. One dramatic effect of this was to increase the proportion of the population enrolled in university study to unprecedented heights — about 20% in England and Wales, and higher still in Scotland. It also changed the status of a large number of educational institutions. Now the former Polys had the right to award degrees according to standards set by themselves, they could appoint professors (which they did in large numbers), and could join the Committee of Vice-Chancellors and Principals. Even more importantly, they entered into direct competition for financial support from the University Funding Councils.

Universities and the State

These funding councils, also set up by the Education Reform Act of 1988, were themselves the outcome of an important part of the history of universities in Britain. Whatever university autonomy may mean, it does not mean, and never meant, freedom from state interference. Almost from the beginning, governments interested themselves in the universities. Early on Oxford and Cambridge colleges were patronized by kings and barons, and the University of Aberdeen, founded more than 500 years ago, was the protégé of James IV, King of Scots, who saw it as a small but important element in the establishment of political independence from the Holy Roman Empire. Edinburgh, whose founders were Presbyterians and consequently lent no credence to the authority of the Pope, turned to James VI of Scotland (later James I of England), for its official sanction.

The role of the state in the provision of higher education has in fact been continuous. All the ancient universities — Oxford, Cambridge, Dublin, St Andrews, Glasgow and Aberdeen were beneficiaries of grants of money and the bestowing of privileges on the part of the Crown, including in several cases the award of 'copyright library' status, which entitled the holder to receive free a copy of every book published in Britain. Nor was this all. From time to time they were also subject to regulation and direct control. Many Regius Chairs — professorial appointments made by (or at least subject to the approval of) the monarch, and which still exist — came into being in an attempt by government to counteract academic nepotism. In the middle of the nineteenth century, the state of the universities in Scotland was believed to have sunk so low that a Royal Commission of inquiry was established. As a consequence of its deliberations, Parliament passed the Universities of Scotland Act of 1858, determining from outside just how they would be organized and run. The Act (with amendments) continues to govern their powers and structure to this day.

These are salutary facts for anyone inclined to think that the thraldom of academia to government is of recent date, and that university autonomy requires a completely 'hands-off' approach on the part of the state. In Britain there is only one wholly independent university, the University of Buckingham. Buckingham deliberately eschews all forms of dependence on state finance. This has secured it a certain sort of freedom. On the other hand, it has made little impression on British university life as a whole, and it should be noted that it too was dependent upon the government to grant it a charter for the awarding of degrees.

The truth is history shows that the state will interest itself in anything that is of social and cultural importance. This observation is two sided. If universities are institutions of consequence, they must expect government interference; freedom from such interference means that they are of no consequence.

A more accurate assessment is that the singular, almost exclusive dependence of universities upon the Exchequer is of relatively recent date. It is not as relative as many think, however. The University Grants Commission (UGC) was set up in 1921, before the establishment of several red brick universities and well in advance of the plate glass and the former polytechnics. At first the amount of money distributed was small in relation to the other funds universities had at their disposal, and the UGC was so constituted that it would provide a buffer between government and higher education, a way of protecting the independence of the latter from the purse-strings of the former. Though the UGC's total budget was set by the Treasury, the distribution between individual universities was not. Moreover, the Committee's being composed in large part of academics was meant to ensure that distribution was based on academic merit, not political favouritism. For quite a time it appeared to work well, though the proportion of university income that came from government grew steadily. After Robbins this steady growth became a flood. Established as well as new universities gratefully received a huge increase in resources. It flowed from other sources also, namely the increasingly important Research Councils who provided financial support for both postgraduate students and for academic research programmes in medicine, engineering, science and social studies. It would not be inaccurate to say that during this period, with a few exceptions (the wealthy Oxbridge colleges), for the first time British universities became completely dependent on the state's largesse — through student fees (paid by local government but reclaimed from central government), statutory grant from central government via the UGC, and research money, again from central government, via the Research Councils.

All these sources of support diminished somewhat in the 1970's. Then serious reductions came, in the 1980's, when the government of Margaret Thatcher resolved that state spending had reached unmanageable proportions, and that every sector would have to bear its share of reducing public expenditure. Moreover, all beneficiaries should be held to account for the effective use of the funds they received.

There followed a period of retrenchment. The UGC made suggestions to individual universities for closure and contraction and many of these were put into effect. Though in theory independent of government policy, the UGC capped student numbers and recommended management reform and other initiatives very much in keeping with the political current of the times. The universities responded with a striking degree of compliance. Believing their survival to depend on the restoration of government support, over the next decade they made immense and important changes, many of which will be considered in more detail in later chapters. Their compliant attitude did not win them political favour, however. Arguably the important Education Reform Act of 1988 took little account of what had happened, or of the views and wishes of university teachers. However this may be, by licensing the conversion of polytechnics to universities it hugely expanded the numbers attending universities, while at the same time setting up a new system of finance – separate Funding Councils for England and Wales, Scotland, and Northern Ireland. These Councils had not much more money to distribute but many more claimants. They also had significantly greater powers of initiative and review than the old UGC had had.

There were three ways in which the new Higher Education Funding Councils came to exercise central control on universities as a whole. The first was through funding initiatives, in which sums of money were set aside for specific areas of student recruitment, teaching or research, and awarded largely by competition, the terms of which were set by the Councils. In this a pattern was being followed which had been set by the Research Councils. The second was by extending an innovation of the UGC's, namely periodic Research Assessment Exercises. These set up subject panels whose task was to judge which universities were producing the best research and scholarship so that they could be rewarded accordingly. The third was the introduction of Teaching Quality Assessment. Here too subject panels were established which, unlike the Research Assessment panels, included external representatives of commerce and industry as well as academic members, and their task was to determine how well institutions were providing for the teaching of the subjects they professed.

Thus in a very short time, though there had emerged no formal equivalent for universities of Her Majesty's Inspectorate of Schools, and despite the fact that universities remained in theory autonomous bodies, they had been forged into a state 'system' largely paid for by the state and subject to extensive central control.

It is important to observe that within fifteen years or so, British universities had been changed very significantly, and though the attitude on behalf of the universities themselves was largely one of passive compliance, very many of those who had served university education and research diligently and well objected profoundly to the changes that had come about and believed them to be largely detrimental and possibly irreversible. It was common to hear the complaint that from being possibly the best in the world, the British University was now at most second rate. We are not for the moment directly concerned with the justice of this complaint, but only with observing that it was widely made, and in part confirmed by the so-called 'brain drain' in which leading academics, and especially scientists, took other posts abroad, notably in the United States. The size of this 'brain drain' tended to be exaggerated, but there is little doubt that many first rate academics, either by emigration or through extensive early retirement schemes, left a system which had ceased to command their respect, still less enthusiasm. Furthermore, the changes that had taken place must have been evident to generations of graduates who had benefited from a collection of universities which, unlike those in most other countries, offered a fairly uniform, and high, standard of education to everyone who gained entry to them. Why then did the changes take place without significant public or political complaint, and why did the radical 1988 Act meet with only minimal resistance from the official Opposition? The answer lies in the fact that the autonomy, reform and financing of universities were not issues of any electoral significance. And the reason for this lay not so much in the actual character of British universities as in their public image.

The Public Image of the University

In democratic politics, there is reason to think, it is how things are widely perceived, not how they are, which is of crucial importance. Few people have the time, interest or ability to look into the complex matters of historical and social fact which rational decision-making requires. In a representative democracy, accordingly, for the most part these things are left to elected legislators and professional civil servants. But at regular intervals, as a check upon authoritarian excess, governments are subject to the popular vote. No doubt, as Winston Churchill famously remarked, this is a bad system — but all others are worse. At any rate it is how things are. When elections come, parties prepare manifestos, but very few read them. Nor do many voters take the trouble to inform themselves about the issues. Rather, they cast their votes on the basis of a mixture of traditional loyalties and popular images, impressions and ideas formed from what they see and read in a wide range of media.

It is a serious mistake to think that these media are all in the business of informing. It is probably true that nowadays people take their ideas of the political issues confronting them almost exclusively from television, newspapers, books and magazines. Certainly attendance at lectures, talks and political meetings is very low. But these media contain far more than the relatively dispassionate recounting of pertinent acts. This is not a claim about secret conspiracies, wilful distortion or hidden agendas. It is just true that modern media contain a great deal by way of visual images, story telling and dramatic representation. It seems likely to me that such things have always played an important part in social and political life. Certainly they have done so for a very long time; the political cartoon has a venerable history. In any event, their role in contemporary opinion forming is considerable. Accordingly, though this is an hypothesis, it is plausible to think that if we want to find the principal influences on most people's understanding of universities in the last few decades we should look to works of fiction rather than recitations of fact. It is not the reports of select committees, royal commissions or statistical investigations, which few read or have access to, but popular images which have had most influence, reinforced by news reporting whose wholly understandable concern is not merely to inform, but to attract and hold an audience.

There is reason, I think, to believe that five highly successful novels contributed enormously to the public perception of British universities. These were Kingsley Amis's *Lucky Jim*, Tom Sharpe's *Porterhouse Blue*, Malcolm Bradbury's *The History Man* and David Lodge's *Changing Places*, followed by *Small World*. The impact of *Porterhouse Blue* and *The History Man* was specially marked since these were adapted with great success for television. What is striking about this collection is that it is, so to speak, comprehensive; it covers the full range of institutions which comprised the British universities of the early 1970's. *Porterhouse Blue* is set in an Oxbridge college, *Lucky Jim* in a red brick, and *The History Man* teaches sociology in a new university of the 60's. Lodge's two novels have an international setting. *Changing Places* contrasts British and American universities, not, in the end, to the advantage of the former, and *Small World* is an amusing mockery of the pretensions of the career intellectual on the international conference circuit.

These are all satires. The successful satirist, it has been said, must be in love with his victim. This is probably true of each of these writers (if Amis could ever have been said to be in love with anything), and it explains why they found some of their most enthusiastic readers amongst academics themselves. But the effect of the satire is likely to be different upon those less well acquainted with and hence less attached to the object of scorn. Taken together, in fact, they presented an attitude of relentless ridicule towards the diverse range of British universities, and limitless ammunition for their enemies, further compounded by the popular, and repeated, television series *A Very Peculiar Practice*. Like all good caricatures these imaginative works bore a striking if highly exaggerated relation to the reality they pilloried, but those who knew little of and had no reason to value the real work and purposes of universities, were not in a position to assess the degree of exaggeration.

The result, in my view, was the creation of an image which could only attract antipathy on the part of politicians and the voting public. This attitude was strengthened by news reports throughout the 1960's of student protest and rebellion, culminating at one point in an attack upon the Queen at the University of Stirling. Any reasonable person, faced with heavy taxation and cuts in public expenditure, and at the same time unfamiliar with universities and the values they embodied, would be driven to question their claims on the public purse, or at least support demands for greater accountability.

So it was that the protests of academics in the 1980's, which were in any case both mixed and muted, fell upon deaf ears. The mixed nature of their message, as it seems to me, arose from two sources. First, there was serious anxiety, one might almost say panic, about how to cope with the end of a regime in which their jobs were secure and the flow of resources to support them seemingly unlimited. Second, there was deep uncertainty about what exactly it was that they could say in their own defence. What *were* universities for? Why *should* society at large value them? Was there not *something* to be said for radical revision and review?

These are all good, if unsettling questions. The fact is, however, that in what the Book of Common Prayer calls the "changes and chances of this fleeting world" they have as yet been unanswered. The universities of Britain have been blown hither and thither by modularization, semesterization, academic audit, quality assurance, staff appraisal, resource allocation modelling, on-line management, student evaluation, research assessment and countless other 'initiatives'. What they have not done is to deploy their own intellectual resources to take critical stock of these changes. Consequently, they have not exhibited that very critical independence which must lie at the heart of their rationale. The point of subsequent chapters is to try to repair this deficiency, to ask what makes a university education worthwhile, what the value of academic research is, and what light the values both of these central functions embody might throw upon the changes that have been imposed upon universities. The hope is that arriving at answers to these questions might contribute something to the crucial task of restoring to institutions of higher education a formative role in their own future.

To address these topics properly it is necessary to step back from the immediacy of contemporary concern and ask some rather more fundamental questions.

CHAPTER 2

Explaining the Value of University Education

Training versus Education

What is a university for? When Pope Alexander IV granted a Bull for the establishment of a university in Old Aberdeen, he set out the hopes that James IV of Scotland (or more probably his adviser Bishop Elphinstone) had for such a place.

> Now, a petition lately presented to us on the part of our dearest son in Christ, James, illustrious king of Scots, desiring that the condition of his people be improved, and considering that in the north-eastern parts of the said kingdom there are some places, separated from the rest of his kingdom by arms of the sea and very high mountains, in which dwell men who are rude, ignorant of letters and almost barbarous and who, on account of the over great distance from the places in which universities flourish and the dangerous passage to such places, cannot have leisure for the study of letters, nay, are so ignorant of these letters that suitable men cannot be found not only for the preaching of the Word of God to the people of those places, but even for the administering of the sacraments; and that if in the famous city of Old Aberdeen, which is near enough to the places foresaid, there should flourish a university in every lawful faculty, very many men of the said kingdom, and especially those parts, would apply themselves to such study of letters and acquire that most precious pearl of knowledge, the ignorant would be informed, and the rude become learned.

The rather splendid wording of this, and the faith it expresses in the sheer power of education, may serve to disguise the striking similarity it bears to what might be said in favour of starting a university nowadays. It cannot be disputed that the modern university is a very different place to the mediaeval one. No modern British university any longer offers courses in canon law, theology is a minor not a major subject, and the medicine taught today has been transformed from the sort of study with which it began almost out of all recognition, thanks to relatively recent advances in the biological and chemical sciences. Nevertheless, the Papal Bull conveys a twofold aim — the training of professionals and the advancement of learning. In other words, from the start Aberdeen, in common with all other universities of similar age, had a dual purpose — vocational training, and education for its own sake. It provided doctors, lawyers and priests, and it gave the populace the opportunity to obtain 'the most precious pearl of knowledge' in the form of an education in the liberal arts. Its service to the locality therefore (and this relation is also an important part of the rationale of its foundation) was both to provide for what we now call manpower needs and to civilize.

What this fact reveals, I think, is that a certain sort of purism about universities is not only out of place, but was never in place. It has sometimes been suggested that the distinguishing mark of universities, as opposed to other institutions of further and higher education, is their concern with knowledge and the pursuit of learning for their own sake, not for the sake of some external practical end. This is in fact Newman's claim in *The Idea of a University*. In my view Newman has not infrequently been misunderstood on this point. The contrast he draws between "education" and what he calls "instruction" is a subject that will be examined in greater detail in the next chapter. However, it must be admitted that there is an interpretation of what he says plausible enough for some people to have claimed his support for the contention that the distinction between study in and for itself and study for the purpose of acquiring a skill or a training is what originally marked the difference between universities and polytechnics, a distinction which, the same way of thinking maintains, has been catastrophically blurred by the merger of the two sectors.

But Aberdeen's Papal Bull, which is wholly representative of its period, shows that even the most ancient universities were centrally engaged in practical training and only partly concerned with the pursuit of learning for its own sake. The training they offered, it is true, was for the professions, not for practitioners of what later became known as 'the mechanical arts'. The significance of this point is one to which we will return. For the moment, it is important to note that at least one familiar contrast — between practical and non-practical study — does not by itself illuminate the distinctiveness of the traditional university. Accordingly, the difference between university and other forms of education is less likely to be located in the difference between practical knowledge and theoretical inquiry than in the difference between, say, training as a mechanic and studying the law. However, to make much headway with uncovering this difference, which will not be addressed directly until Chapter 3, we need to turn to more abstract topics.

When Plato wanted to explore the proper ordering of a human life he first examined the proper ordering of society, believing that if we can determine what is good and right on the larger social scale, we will be able to see more clearly what a properly ordered life for the individual might be. The idea that society should be an analogue for understanding the individual soul strikes us as curious because now, and for a long time, our tendency has been to think of these things the other way about. We are inclined to conceive of and talk about the conduct of society, and more especially the state, as if it were an individual agent, and we seek to understand it accordingly. There are good (if somewhat vexed) arguments to think that this is an important and far-reaching error, but these need not concern us directly here, though something more will be said about them in due course. It is enough, for the moment, to explore one aspect of this analogy and draw out some of the implications it is commonly thought to have for the idea of a university education. It can be shown, I think, that there is a good deal of confusion surrounding these implications, and that some of the confusion arises precisely from the employment of the analogy.

The Useful and the Valuable

The activities of any individual can be divided into two broad categories — work and leisure. There are other distinctions with which this can be (but ought not to be) confused. The distinction between work and leisure is not that between the dreary and the pleasurable, for instance. Some people find their work a source of great personal satisfaction and others find that leisure activities can pall. Nor is it a distinction between employment and non-employment. The possessor of vast inherited wealth, who is not employed, is working, in the relevant sense, when he keeps track of his millions or draws more money from the bank. Similarly, the unemployed in receipt of social security are working, in this same sense, when they stand in line to collect their benefit or fill in the forms bureaucracy requires. The distinction between work and leisure, then, is really between those activities that are necessary to live, and those which make living valuable or worthwhile. We might express this distinction as one between useful activities (work) and valuable activities (leisure). Any given activity, of course, even in the life of one individual, may be both useful and valuable, but there must always be some such distinction just because we can always ask of any activity (or object) that is useful – what is it useful for? – and because we can always ask this question, we need some further evaluative conception which will answer it, and which is not itself open to the very same question. It is this further conception that I am calling 'the valuable'. In short, every human life will contain actions and objects whose purpose is to sustain life, and others whose purpose is to make life worth sustaining.

If, returning to our analogy, we think of society as in some sense an entity on a par with individuals, we find, or seem to find, a similar distinction, sometimes thought of as the distinction between productive and non-productive activities, but better expressed as the distinction between wealth-creating and wealth-consuming activities. By analogy, then, just as an individual can only go to the theatre if he has done enough 'work' to give him the price of his ticket, so a society can only afford to support theatricals if it has produced the goods and services that will allow it to pay for them.

If this is indeed so, it appears to imply that social policy must give a certain priority to wealth-creation. We need to create wealth before we can consume it, and how much we have available for consumption will depend on how much we have created. It is on the basis of this implication, very often, that countries are said by their political leaders not to be able to afford this or that. The distinction between wealth-creation and wealth-consumption however, even in its own terms, is a little too simple. There are obviously activities which, though not directly wealth-creating, nevertheless contribute to wealth-creating capacity. Adam Smith regarded preaching and religious ministration in this way, as contributing to productive ability rather than directly to production. A more plausible example nowadays might be medicine; healthy people are more productive than sick people, and it is in this way doctors contribute to general well-being. Education and research can also be thought of along these lines. On this understanding, education and research are not themselves wealth-creating, but the former gives individuals the skills to create wealth, and the latter explores and opens up further possibilities of wealth-creation.

It is evident, to my mind, that the distinction I have been elaborating provides the terms in which many contemporary political and social questions are construed and discussed, most especially in the conduct of schools and universities. Just as an individual must ensure that his or her expenditure does not consistently and over a long period exceed income, so a society must ensure that the money and effort devoted to wealth-consuming activities do not consistently and over a long period exceed those devoted to wealth-creating activities. Further, if opportunities for wealth-consumption are to be expanded, wealth-creating capacity must be expanded also and, for a time at least, an adjustment made between the two activities — just as an individual will work overtime to pay for a more exciting holiday, or take evening classes to advance his wage- or salary-earning potential.

It is this idea of 'adjustment' which dominated government policy with respect to universities in Britain throughout most of the 1980's, and provided the framework in which almost all parties to the debate on this policy were inclined to think about it. If, adopting my earlier terminology, we call wealth-creating activities 'useful' and those activities in which wealth ought to be consumed 'valuable', we can describe the policy of adjustment as a shift from the valuable to the useful, and the political debate as a debate about the appropriate magnitude of this shift.

Now, viewed in this light, not all university subjects are useful. Some are, so to speak, 'practical', some are not, and others occupy an uncertain middle ground. Most who speak in this way would agree that civil engineering and computing science are useful subjects, while classics and archaeology, however valuable, are not, while economics and geography will have supporters and opponents on the ground of their usefulness. Similarly, research will be classified as 'applied' and 'pure', another version of the same distinction to be discussed more directly in a later chapter. And there will be disputes about which subjects (especially among the natural sciences) within the general category of the 'pure' have practical potential and which do not.

Transferable Skills

Once the policy of 'adjustment' is accepted, not just as a policy to be applied within universities, or even education, but between different areas of public expenditure, it obviously becomes extremely important to distinguish between 'useful' and 'non-useful' subjects and areas of research. It also becomes tempting for academics to try to connect their subjects with the conception of 'usefulness' even at the cost of using rather strained (and occasionally, it must be said, contemptible) arguments. It is against this background in fact that the language of 'transferable skills' has gained the great credence it has. In the belief that education in some of the subjects universities teach is not in itself 'useful', and so not easily given a convincing public justification, very many institutions have come to require that course proposals should list the 'transferable skills' that students are expected to gain from them. So, for instance, courses in classics or philosophy or mediaeval history are advertised as worth taking in part because of the (generalized) intellectual discipline and literary skills they inculcate.

Now if we are to secure an adequate explanation of the value of university education, it is crucial to observe that justification in terms of transferable skills offers no support whatever for the *content* of these subjects. From the point of view of transferable skills, any 'useful' subject, such as engineering or pharmacology, which *also* teaches mental discipline, could, and should, replace classics or philosophy without remainder. The point is not that there are no transferable skills. It may indeed be the case, as has often been claimed, that a training in the classics inculcates habits of mind which are of great service in the sort of work that members of the higher civil service are required to do. The error in the appeal to transferable skills does not lie in its falsehood, but in the fact that it attempts to explain value in terms of use. A direct parallel is this: perhaps learning to play the piano makes people more adept at chopping vegetables, but it could only be a certain sort of desperation that made a musician explain the value of the former in terms of the usefulness of the latter. The general point is this: If the useful alone is valuable, subjects which are not in themselves useful can only have derivative, never intrinsic value, and hence such value as they possess can be derived in other, more directly useful ways.

The protagonists of classics, philosophy, Egyptology, Sanskrit or art history who adopt the language of transferable skills need to think again. But there are other ways in which they can think. The first step in formulating an alternative to this 'second-hand' justification of their existence is for practitioners of traditional 'academic' subjects to grasp that making these gestures of conciliation in the direction of the 'useful' is unnecessary. There is no need to make such a concession at all.

Usefulness

Are there any subjects which are, in themselves, useful or useless? The answer is 'No'. This is not because one never knows what might not turn out to be useful, a thought upon which the defence of 'pure' scientific inquiry has not infrequently relied. The real reason is rather that 'useful' is a relative term; something has to be useful *for* something or other. The contemporary obsession with usefulness, in this respect, mirrors the sixties obsession with 'relevance'. Subjects have to be relevant *to* something; there is no such thing as relevance *per se*. Similarly, since people's purposes differ, there is no such thing as 'usefulness' in the abstract; everything useful must be useful *for* something. This is easiest to see if we consider specific examples. Cancer research, for instance, is often taken to be paradigmatic of 'useful' scientific investigation. However, the results of cancer research are no use whatever to those whose business is improving agriculture or reducing the number of traffic accidents, though these are equally laudable aims from the point of view of ameliorating the human condition. Conversely, the mastery of ancient Greek is usually thought of as 'useless'. In fact, it is not merely useful, but essential, for those who want to study Plato in the original language.

These examples make the essentially relative character of usefulness thoroughly obvious, but they are sometimes resisted in the belief that the point is merely a verbal one, one about the meaning of the word 'useful'. Importantly, this is not so. We are concerned here with conceptual issues, not grammatical ones. Compare the study of Latin with the study of French. Knowledge of French is often thought to have a usefulness that a knowledge of Latin does not, which in part explains why modern languages have displaced ancient ones in most schools. But it is a matter of incontestable fact that if one's purpose is to read Ovid, to enter the Roman Curia, or to be a teacher of classical literature, a knowledge of French is of no more use than a knowledge of Swahili. Claims about the usefulness of modern languages are sometimes sustained by the idea, or assumption perhaps, that knowledge of French is *more* useful than knowledge of Latin. If there cannot be usefulness in the abstract, however, there cannot be degrees of usefulness. Such claims can only be taken to mean that there are more purposes for which French is useful than there are for Latin.

It is hard to know how, for means of comparison, the number of purposes a specific body of knowledge or skill serves is to be counted up, but even if it is true that some serve more purposes than others, this fact is of no interest to actual people until it has been shown that this wider range of purposes contains more of the purposes that they may (or may reasonably be expected to) have. With a knowledge of French one can *both* holiday in France more satisfactorily *and* read the literature of the country, whereas with Latin one can only read the literature; it does not help with holidays in Italy. This is true, but it does not make French any more 'useful' to those who always holiday in the Highlands of Scotland and wish to read Latin poetry or study the origins of Roman law.

The conclusion to be drawn in the present context is that as far as individuals are concerned, it is not possible to generalize about usefulness in such a way that we could divide university subjects into the 'useful' and the 'useless'. The simple truth is that any subject may be useful to some people for certain purposes, and useless to others for others. What we can often say, for limited periods of time, is that certain subjects are more likely to be useful to a larger number of people than other subjects are. The central question for the topic of this chapter is why, in explaining the value of universities, special attention should be paid to this fact.

One answer is that the propensity of a subject to be useful to a larger number of people makes it socially more valuable. With this suggestion we move from the individual to society, and hence return to the analogy that is commonly made between them.

If the foregoing analysis is correct, some subjects at some times can be described as being more useful for more purposes to more people than others. It is under the influence of this thought that information processing, it is frequently suggested, is more useful than other subjects. IT is useful in very many different ways, whereas archaeology, for example, is useful to only a few people in a few ways. Thus expressly stated, however, we should not let this truth impress us unduly. There seems little doubt that the comparison of mortgage and other interest rates is likely to be of use to far more people than the study of Anglo-Saxon. Would this warrant our replacing the latter with the former in university curricula? Before we could reasonably draw this conclusion we would need, in addition to an assessment of the greater usefulness of a subject in the sense just specified, to arrive at some assessment of the value of the purposes for which it is useful.

Consider this example. In terms of multiplicity of uses, food science can be thought more useful than many other subjects. It often *is* more useful, in fact. But we cannot conclude that it is more *valuable* until we have put its investigations and results in a larger context. If the greater usefulness of food science were to lie in its ability to provide manufacturers with the means to increase the number of flavours of crisps, instant puddings or scented erasers, further argument is needed to show that these advances are especially valuable. Perhaps we have an enormous number of such flavours already (which indeed we do), and, as the (somewhat misnamed) principle of diminishing marginal utility tells us, further additions of more generate very little by way of added value. Where this is the case, we have good reason to resist all attempts to devote greater resources to food science. Largely, it has given us all it has to give and the admitted usefulness of yet more does not generate much, if anything at all, in the way of value.

These observations, plainly stated, seem self-evident, yet they fly in the face of a widely held belief that it is possible to employ a general basis of assessment which will enable us to distinguish between the more and the less useful. This general basis is usually thought to be wealth-creation. The widespread belief is that a subject may be described as more useful, that is to say, one which serves more purposes for more people, if it can be shown to be part of the social process of wealth-creation. Conversely it is less useful if it can be shown to be part of social consumption.

Wealth Creation

The concept of wealth-creation is complex. It is sufficient for present purposes, however, to draw attention to certain misunderstandings which surround it, and which are of the greatest importance for understanding the nature and value of a university education. First, it is clearly wrong to think that wealth-creation is the earning of money. To begin with, the creation of wealth is possible in a barter economy, and is even possible where there is no economy at all — a hermit may create wealth, that is, make his life richer than it was by means of his own labour. Secondly, it is wrong to think of wealth-creation as the manufacture of saleable goods. The life of the individual may also be enriched, in a perfectly straightforward sense, by the composition of music, the learning of games, the advancement of knowledge and understanding, and enjoyment of the natural environment. Thirdly, it is wrong to think of wealth-creation as an increase in the normal means of procuring goods and services. A society can have extensive financial reserves but its members, in the main, be unable to enrich their lives because the schools, roads, hospitals, universities, museums, theatres and sports facilities do not exist in which these reserves could be spent. Such has been the case in many Arab countries with immense oil revenues, but relatively little to spend them on.

In short, it is wrong to think of wealth-creation as the generation of income, even in the case of the individual in the abstract. In practice for many people income, provided it can be spent, *is* a measure of wealth, and an increase in income accordingly a measurable increase in wealth, but it is wrong to think of it in this way as far as society is concerned — for two reasons. Not only is an increase in purchasing power not of itself an increase in wealth, but a society is composed of many members amongst whom money and goods circulate, and between whom wealth is *exchanged*. The process of exchange, unlike the simple acquisition of the hermit, involves the creation and consumption of wealth simultaneously. To put it crudely, the very same five pound note which I spend, you earn, whenever we trade goods or services. Wealth-creation and wealth-consumption, in a *social* context, are simply the same action viewed from two different sides and since, as economists have told us for long enough, the very act of exchange may itself create additional wealth, it is senseless to speak of the two as in opposition.

What is the bearing of all this on the use and value of universities as social institutions? We have seen that from the point of view of specific individuals with certain purposes, some university subjects may be more useful than others. We have also seen that some subjects may be of use to more individuals than others, but that this, by itself, does not give us reason to value them more highly. To discriminate between subjects or educational institutions in the way that is commonly done, we need to be able to show that, just as an individual must work before he can play, a society must put wealth-creation before consumption, and that subjects are to be determined 'useful' as they contribute to wealth-creation. What the foregoing analysis shows is that this attempt rests upon a misunderstanding of wealth-creation in a social context. It follows that any attempt to discriminate in general between useful and useless subjects, or between wealth-creating and wealth-consuming intellectual activities is groundless. No subject can be declared useless (or useful) in the abstract, and all serious intellectual inquiry, I believe, can be declared valuable in terms of wealth-creation. This conclusion is confirmed, if we examine carefully some familiar objections to it.

Utilitarian Suppositions

The points I have made in support of these contentions about usefulness and wealth creation do not rely on any very novel insights. On the contrary, it is an important part of the strategy of this chapter that they consist largely in commonplaces, albeit commonplaces which have been frequently overlooked. They have been overlooked because of the strongly utilitarian presuppositions that have governed the discussion of these issues for some considerable time. For instance, from a utilitarian point of view it seems obvious that we could all be farmers, but we could not all be philosophers and that consequently some occupations are necessary and others a luxury. But is this so obvious? Actually, once one thinks about it, it seems obviously *false*. "Man cannot live by bread alone", since at a minimum he also needs stones that have been specially fashioned with which to grind the flour and firewood that has been gathered with which to bake the dough. This was not, of course, the point Moses was making, which was rather that there are other and perhaps more important forms of wealth than bread. "Man cannot live by bread alone" need not be interpreted as a sententious or otherworldly appeal to the spiritual, however. A society in which all are hunters, herders and gatherers is, quite literally, a poorer society than one in which there are also musicians, philosophers and actors. The important point to grasp about this observation is that the music and the philosophy are not *bought* with a richer society's wealth, but are themselves *part* of it.

Might it not be said, nonetheless, that there is an undeniable difference between those things that are fundamentally necessary for human life and those that are not? Surely food is needed in a sense in which classical learning is not? The difference between food and knowledge is real, but it is not significant for the topic under discussion. No one could plausibly suggest that the difference between 'useful' and 'useless' subjects or activities lies in the capacity of the former to supply basic needs. We could live without classical learning, it is true, but so we could without computers, telephones, railway timetables and vaccines, all of them paradigmatically 'useful'. None of these things is needed just to keep life going. But any of them can play an essential part in making life qualitatively more valuable. Classical learning may be unnecessary from the point of view of basic subsistence, but it is not any more so than computational science. It follows that basic subsistence cannot provide a point of view from which to adjudicate between the value of these two subjects.

It is tempting, even while conceding these points, to cling to the belief that there is *some* difference here which, presumably, has not yet been properly articulated. This residual belief might be expressed, as it commonly is, in the claim that society needs farmers and mechanics, whereas it does not, strictly, need historians or sculptors. This is a claim of the greatest interest, I think, because while it is a way of thinking that powerfully influences public policy and discussion, it is also one that is deeply mistaken.

The Needs of Society

To begin with, the idea that we could need, say, engineers without needing non-engineers is absurd. We only need roads if we have reason to travel, and if our sole reason were to explore further possibilities for road building the whole exercise would be pointlessly circular. Road engineers are valuable because, amongst other things, we want to drive to the opera, visit friends or attend lectures on Egyptology. Similarly, electrical engineering is useful only in so far as its serves needs other than itself — lighting the places in which we live and work, making possible films and television programmes which have independent value. In short, society *needs* such skills only in so far as the individuals who comprise it *want* other things, things that non-engineers supply.

A second point to be made is this: the individuals who make up society have different wants and hence different needs. Earlier it was shown that some subjects serve some of these needs, and other subjects others. Consequently, to declare one group of subjects more useful than another is implicitly to declare a preference for the purposes they happen to serve. To put it bluntly: to maintain that electronic engineering is useful in comparison with musicology is to declare a preference for, amongst other things, video games over composition or concert going. Even this way of putting the point is misleading. The opposition between the two is quite factitious; one reason for valuing electronic engineering lies in its usefulness for the recording of music.

But in any case, on what are such selective preferences to be based? One answer, consonant with the utilitarian line of thought we have been examining, is that 'society', over and above the individuals who at any time comprise it, needs one more than the other. (If it did, then presumably it would pay them more. One reason to doubt the utilitarian assumption lies in the fact that it does not.) But to speak in this way is to think of society as an individual, the analogy with which we began, and to which we must now return. Margaret Thatcher's unguarded remark that 'There is no such thing as Society' met with much ridicule, in part rightly so, since it is easily shown that a society is not identical with the people who comprise it. The population of any society changes constantly, because of births and deaths, and though societies can indeed come to an end, they do not do so just because their population changes. If they did, their existence would be fleeting indeed. Still, it does not follow that 'Society' is the sort of entity which can be said to have needs or desires independently of the needs and desires of those who comprise it. It is only human beings who desire things, and hence only human beings who need the means to satisfy those desires. Whatever sort of thing society may properly be said to be, its 'needs' cannot be appealed to independently of the generalised needs of human beings. Besides, even if they could, 'Society' cannot sensibly be said, except metaphorically, to have a voice or hands. It takes individuals to declare the needs of 'Society' and to do its bidding. Who are we to take as its spokesmen?

Politicians are particularly prone to speak on behalf of 'Society', but industrialists and commercial interests, who more often speak of 'the economy', have been quick to do the same thing. Now it is these spokesmen, amongst others, who have for some time set the terms on which the social value of universities is assessed. Their view, however, is partial. This is not the same as saying it is prejudiced, though it may be. The point to be emphasized is that both politicians and industrialists have special interests, and that it is a mistake to think of their interests as being, or even indirectly representing, the interests of all. To arrive at a more adequate assessment and explanation of the social value of universities (or any other institution for that matter), we have to adopt a more general, less partial view.

Nearly everyone values health and longevity, hence the ease with which the claim that 'Society' needs doctors and health workers meets with general approval. Nearly everyone values recreation and pleasure. Hence the ease with which music and film, despite their largely non-utilitarian character, gain social support. Tastes differ of course, but commercially successful musicals and popular cinema which attracts spontaneous audiences are rarely called upon to justify themselves to others. Health and recreation are importantly different however. Freedom from disease and longevity are worth having only in as far as there are rewarding ways in which long and healthy lives can be spent. To be healthy and long-lived in solitary confinement without any source of stimulation or any means of recreation or diversion is, arguably, a fate worse than death. The importance of recreation and pleasure lies in their ability to supply such a deficiency. Health and longevity are means, amongst other things, to the end of pleasure and enjoyment. In other words, to employ an earlier distinction, health and longevity are useful; pleasure and enjoyment are valuable.

Pleasure, though important and intuitively attractive to most people, is not the only value that makes life worthwhile. Only out and out hedonists would think to the contrary. And this brings us to the principal issue around which the social value of universities turns. If, in the end, what society needs is what makes the individuals who comprise it better off, the question is: what *does* make human beings better off? It should be obvious that the list of those things which enrich a human life goes beyond the crudely utilitarian conception of 'basic' needs. It also goes beyond pleasure and enjoyment and includes knowledge and understanding. Though the slogan 'the value of knowledge for its own sake' is itself misleading, as we shall see in a later chapter, those, like Newman, who espouse it are pointing to an important truth. There is no reason to believe that, in the abstract, health or pleasure are any more enriching than knowledge. It follows that the producers of knowledge enrich human lives, and hence enrich society, no less than the producers of health and pleasure.

When industrialists, and in their wake, politicians, speak of what society needs they are usually referring to the means of increasing prosperity. There is nothing wrong, duplicitous, or necessarily philistine about this. But it needs to be said again and again that the concept of 'prosperity' conceived solely as purchasing power is logically incomplete. It says nothing about what that increased prosperity is to be spent on, and without additional *objects* of consumption, additional *means* of consumption are worthless. Wealth creation, properly understood, requires both. A society is truly richer only if it has *both* the means of securing better lives for its citizens *and* the availability of the objects which make lives better. The terms of the contemporary debate about the value of universities tends to have focused it on the contribution they might make to the means. It has generally ignored the contribution they make to the objects. And academics themselves have been lured into the argument about means, a context in which they can never do full justice to the institutions and activities in which they are engaged.

To assess the value of universities to society, then, we need to look at their contribution to wealth creation without distorting this to imply prosperity in the restricted and incomplete sense it so often has. Viewed in this light, there are two ways in which universities contribute to the societies of which they are a part. The first is education and the second is research. To say this, however, is not to answer the question of their social value, but only to set the context for answering it. This is because so stated, their aims are not unique. Schools and colleges of technology also educate; commercial laboratories and pollsters also engage in research. So why should what goes on in universities be given special attention? If an answer is to be found it must lie in what is distinctive about university education and research. These are the respective topics of the next two chapters.

CHAPTER 3

University Education

Right at the outset of *The Idea of a University*, Cardinal Newman states his main thesis in the plainest possible fashion.

> The view taken of a University in these Discourses is the following: — That it is a place of *teaching* universal *knowledge*. This implies that its object is . . . the diffusion and extension of knowledge rather than the advancement. If its object were scientific and philosophical discovery, I do not see why a University should have students. . . (Newman 1982: xxxvii, emphasis original)

This contention is at odds with the self-professed (and government encouraged) conception of the modern British university, in which research is seen as at least as important, and sometimes more so, than teaching. Yet with the exception of very special institutions such as All Souls College, Oxford, British universities exist in large measure to educate those who register in them as students, and depend heavily upon the support of the public purse as providers of university education. Arguably then, whatever the merits of research, the topic of the next chapter, education is an ineliminable part of a university's function.

I use the term 'university education' for the topic of this chapter because the more common expression 'higher education' is unsatisfactory in at least one important respect; it does not attribute any distinctiveness to studying at university rather than other places of tertiary education. British English used to employ a terminological distinction that has largely been lost in contemporary parlance. At one time those who attended schools were known as pupils and those who attended institutions of higher education were known as students. Partly under the influence of American English, the two terms have recently converged and those attending schools are as likely to be referred to as students. The matter is not merely linguistic however. The adoption of the term 'student' to refer to those in secondary, and even primary education, also signals a change in educational philosophy, a belief that self-motivated inquiry is more appropriate for schoolchildren too, more appropriate that is to say than mere passive reception of 'lessons'.

The truth or falsity of this belief lies at the heart of contemporary concern with school education. It is not my purpose to examine the issue here, however. All that needs to be noticed for present purposes is that this important tenet of educational theory, whether cogent or not, can only be stated if it employs the same important difference which the older usage marked, namely that whereas pupils are taught, students study. Though nothing turns on mere terminology, I shall make use of the traditional distinction between pupils and students to explore what there is to be said about the distinctiveness of a university education.

Students and Pupils

It is the *conceptual* difference between studying and being taught which is most worth uncovering for present purposes. Though it is not often made explicit in these terms, it is frequently evident in the practical experience of the individuals who cease to be pupils and become students. An important part of this practical experience is that students at colleges and universities find themselves much less subject to educational discipline than when they were pupils at school. It is true that in general the transition from school to higher education can be difficult, and this for a number of reasons. Chief among these, perhaps, is the fact that those making the transition are often leaving their parental homes for the first time. But the nature of their relation to their studies also changes in ways that can be unsettling. First, they are required to spend far less time in class. Second, their attendance is not subject to the scrutiny it was; there are (as yet) no university truant officers. Third, their work is far less directed. Of course there are great variations between institutions in this respect, and indeed between subjects and disciplines. Consequently, generalisation is fraught with risks. Nevertheless, it is broadly true that while *pupils* are for the most part directed by others, *students* are expected to be much more self-directed. There are deadlines for essays, lab reports and so on, to be met, and there are examinations to be passed. But just how these are prepared for is largely a matter for the student to decide.

This element of self-direction can be taken, in fact, as a crucial difference between pupils and students, and hence between schools and colleges. Here too, we might observe, British English and American English diverge somewhat, since, while some British schools are called colleges, it is common for Americans to refer to universities as 'schools', a usage which is still alien in Britain. There is also the fact already noted that many educational theorists would claim that those who are at school should be accorded the status of student (in my sense). Once again, nothing much turns on the words we use, and, to repeat, I do not propose to enter into debates about the objectives that are appropriate for primary and secondary education. I shall simply use the term 'school' to refer to primary and secondary education and 'tertiary education' to refer to the sector within which universities are to be found but which, importantly, they do not wholly encompass.

Tertiary education in this country has a number of distinguishing features. First, participation in it is voluntary. Since the Education Act of 1870, some school education has been compulsory for the nation's children; only the length of time that must be spent at school has altered. Second, tertiary education has always been available, and increasingly so of late, to a variety of ages — not just to the school leaver. Third, and this point, already observed, is one of considerable significance, a large part of tertiary education not only relies upon but strives to inculcate self-directed study. Once more, the lines here are blurred. Colleges of Further Education prepare all ages for relatively low level examinations and modern educational practice in schools has encouraged the technique of active 'discovery' in preference to passive 'learning'. Whether this is for good or ill is an important question, but it is not the issue here. Many have come to reject, or at least question, the theory behind the practice. By contrast, no one seriously doubts that the mastery of autonomous inquiry is a crucial part of 'higher' education. In other words, it is widely agreed that there is a level of education at which a large part of the educator's task is to equip the student with the means to pursue inquiry on his or her own part.

If this is a central feature of tertiary education in general, it cannot be taken to mark out the peculiarities of university education *per se*. What then are these peculiarities? In answering this question we can still learn something from Newman.

Education versus Instruction

Newman's distinction between 'education' and 'instruction' is drawn in order to mark this difference. In amplification of it he contrasts 'the philosophical' with 'the mechanical', the former being characterized by an introduction to 'general ideas', the latter with information "that is exhausted upon what is particular and external". Newman's language sounds odd to our ears, yet what he means to convey is familiar enough. It has to do with the different direction of thought that alternative forms of inquiry take. There is good reason to follow him in his use of the term 'philosophical' because it is philosophy properly so-called in which the direction of the first is most marked. Students (and others) often complain that philosophy is inconclusive. They mean that philosophical reflection never seems to lead to any firm and decisive result. Its direction is such that, far from matters being settled, the longer we engage in philosophical reflection, the more further and larger issues seem to open up. The complaint of inconclusiveness is overstated, in my view, because less attention is paid than it should be to the value of the negative no less than the positive. From the earliest times we find Socrates claiming, in the face of a similar objection, that if he knew nothing positive, he at least knew what he did not know; he knew just how *ignorant* he was. This put him, he thought, at an advantage over many of his contemporaries, who supposed that they knew what they believed, while in reality their beliefs, however firmly held, were groundless.

Knowledge of the negative is still knowledge. It is not just a mark of philosophy, however. Karl Popper made falsification, rather than verification, the mark of real science. He did so, in part, because of the history of science. One of most telling events of this history is the overthrow of Newton by Einstein. Newton seemed to make, and did make, real advances in scientific understanding over the Aristotelian physics that had dominated European thinking for so long. Yet in their turn the conceptions of Newtonian mechanics were, eventually, rendered largely redundant by relativity theory. And we can expect, in due course, that Einstein will also be superseded. It seems that it is the apprehension of the false rather than the true in which progress in scientific understanding consists, which is why Popper chose falsification as the true test of science. It follows that no scientific hypothesis can be taken to be the last word.

We can say something similar of history. While the basic facts of the past can be established with certainty — Louis XIV died in 1715 — the larger story of any period is constantly under review — the full significance of the rule of 'Le Roi Soleil' is still open to revision. In the study of philosophy, natural science and history, then, students are encouraged, in a phrase of Michael Oakeshott's, to 'spread their sails to the argument' without knowing where or to what purpose this might lead. By contrast, the engineer and the pharmacist need to know 'hard' fact, truths which, when we know them are, in Newman's terminology, 'exhausted'. Only so can they be securely acted upon. It is not the business of the practical intelligence to raise general doubts and conceptual difficulties, but to ascertain what is needed for the purpose in hand. Water flows downhill. To know this is enough for the purposes of harnessing its power. Knowledge of the fact exhausts the inquiry. But why *does* water flow downhill? *Must* it be so? These questions lead in a different direction, and when we have a mind to inquire into them, the fact itself becomes one of relatively little interest.

Why, though, should we pursue such questions? What is the point if, in the end, they make us no better at constructing watermills, and hence no better at grinding flour and making bread? The answer, according to Newman, is that the desire to know is as basic a feature of human beings as the desire to do or to have. In my view it is a mistake to express his contention in terms of 'knowledge as its own end' but the defence of this claim must await the next chapter. For the moment it is enough to record that there is substance to his contrast between 'the philosophical' and 'the mechanical'.

Supposing it to be so, the import is this. Those who engage in learning as opposed to instruction are set upon a course — the investigation of general ideas — which in turn implies a different relation between learning and the mind which learns than the relation implied in a process of 'instruction'. There is neither reason nor occasion to mark this difference in terms of respective value. Newman does not claim — and no one needs to — that education is superior to instruction, only that it is different. The tendency to mark the difference with different evaluations has bedevilled debates about higher education. It is a mark of the British educational tradition that the 'academic' has been held in higher esteem than the 'practical', and this prejudice partly explains why polytechnics and colleges of technology were keen to change their names. At the same time prejudice is at work in the other direction also, which is why the 'purely' academic has often felt under a special pressure to justify itself.

It is questionable whether a preference for the 'academic' can be given any rational foundation, and equally questionable whether we should accept the value of the 'practical' at its own estimation. Something has already been said about this, but in any case it is not the issue here. What we want to know, rather, is what the nature and significance of the distinction is, and how it might reflect on the value of university education.

Liberal versus Technical

In exploring these matters further we need to return to an observation made at the start of the last chapter. Since earliest times universities have included within their curricula subjects broadly called 'practical'. The training of priests, lawyers and doctors is as old a part of their purpose as an education in the liberal arts. This is why, unless we disregard a large part of its history, a place must be found within university education for training as well as for learning, for the practical as well as the liberal arts and pure sciences. The distinction we need to elaborate, accordingly, is one which will differentiate between lawyers and mechanics no less than between mechanics and philosophers. It will be useful, therefore, to replace the language of training *versus* education with a different terminology, one which contrasts technical with liberal education.

The expression 'liberal' education comes from the Latin *liberalis*, meaning 'befitting a free man'. It thus implies an education suited to the exercise of citizenry, or social participation in general. This is why Newman contrasts 'liberal' with 'servile' and, he says, "by 'servile' work is understood . . . bodily labour, mechanical employment and the like in which the mind has little or no part" (Newman 1982: 80). 'Servile' is an unattractive term to modern ears, but it is not one we need to invoke in order to acknowledge that there are some technical accomplishments which are almost entirely a matter of inarticulate knack or art. That is to say (in Socratic language), people can master practical techniques while being quite unable to 'give an account' of them, i.e. formulate, or even indicate, the principles that underlie them. There is no reason to denigrate such practical mastery, although Socrates (or Plato perhaps) tended to do so. Straightforward mastery of this sort accurately describes most people's linguistic ability; they can speak a language whose grammatical and linguistic structures they cannot articulate. In a similar fashion, it is generally true that mechanics, plumbers and electricians are masters of inarticulate skills. From the point of view of the purposes such skills are intended to serve this is of no consequence. What we want is that our telephones, taps or lights work. Why should we care if those who can put them to rights cannot explain, except in elementary terms, how they have done so or give a theoretical explanation of why what they have done has been successful? Still less do we count it a deficiency that they have no knowledge of the higher sciences which underlie them. Conversely, as is well known, those versed in electro-dynamics may be quite unable to fix the power supply, botanists do not necessarily make good gardeners and nutritionists may be unable to cook.

Still, though there are these inarticulate skills that are no worse off for their inarticulacy, it is also the case that there are practical tasks the performance of which is improved by the addition of more intellectual accomplishments. In a world of rapidly changing and increasingly sophisticated technology — computer technology is a good example — it is inconceivable that satisfactory results should be achieved through relatively unreflective techniques alone. And so it is that technological education has come more and more to involve its students in theoretical issues which prompt and encourage mental inquisitiveness and imagination. The very term 'technology' implies this, made up as it is of an amalgam of the Greek terms for both skill and explanation. Teachers of technology rightly deny that their task can be restricted to the instilling of mere techniques and accordingly any technology syllabus will have intellectual as well as technical components. This is true of electrical and mechanical engineering. It is even more so of service industry subjects like transportation, management or media studies which, though practical, are not generally thought of as technological.

Does the existence of technology and service industry subjects mean that the distinction between technical and liberal education has been breached, or needs to be abandoned even? In answer to this question it is worth recalling that Newman, the high priest of liberal education, did not deny the power of such subjects to provide intellectual stimulus. On the contrary, he says "no one can deny that commerce and the professions afford scope for the highest and most diversified powers of the mind" (Newman 1982: 81). But if they do, does an education in them not also become liberal on Newman's own interpretation of the term? If it does, is there not reason to favour these over more academic subjects since the former are *both* liberal *and* useful while the latter are liberal only?

This question returns us to a topic of the last chapter — transferable skills. In discussing the move to defend seemingly 'useless' subjects on the grounds of the transferable skills they teach, it was noted that no such defence could satisfactorily explain the value of those subjects with respect to their *content*. And yet it is in their content that an adequate explanation must lie. The same point can be made in other contexts. If we justify football on the strength of its ability to contribute to physical fitness, an ability it undoubtedly has, we say nothing about the special merits of the game itself. A proper approach, though there is space only to sketch it here, must focus first upon the aims of game playing and then explain the distinctive ways in which football gives scope for them, or some of them. Physical fitness, we might say, is a *benefit* which comes of playing football, but it is not the *point* of playing it.

In the same way, literacy, numeracy, articulacy and facility with analysis are benefits (let us hope) of studying philosophy, linguistics, psychology, jurisprudence, comparative religion or cosmology; but it is not in these that we find their point. The point, rather, as I think Newman meant to say, is the exercise and enriching of the life of the mind for its own sake.

But are we any further forward in making this observation? If technological education is in part intellectual and affords 'scope for the highest and most diversified powers of the mind', what argument can be made for the independent value of non-technological subjects? The answer lies, I think, in the fact that the exercise of the powers of the mind which technology requires is *not* required for its own sake, but for the sake of another end. To take a specific instance. Media studies goes beyond the technical mastery of camera work, editing and the like, and it does so because if its purpose is to equip people for a lifetime's work in television and film studios, it must leave them with an intellectual ability to adapt to rapidly changing technology, and with the conceptual imagination to explore and exploit possibilities which simply were unavailable at the time of their training. All this is true, it seems to me, yet the point of such intellectual accomplishments nevertheless lies in their being of service to the as yet unimagined practical tasks of the television and film industry of the future. The life of the mind in such service can be both challenging and stimulating; it is a prejudice to think otherwise. For all that, it is subservient to an external purpose.

The distinguishing mark of liberal arts and pure sciences can now be said to be this. Their point is to enrich the mind, and their value lies in the success with which they do this. Importantly, however, they cannot be said to do this by means of the disciplines they inculcate. This, we have seen, is a feature they share with technological subjects. It follows that their peculiar powers of intellectual enrichment lie in their content. It is not that they provide occasions for thought, which they do, but that they provide the most worthwhile *objects* of thought. It is here that the rationale of university education properly so called lies; it is a source of wealth *per se*.

Is this true? The answer depends upon two propositions, first that intellectual enrichment is indeed a form of wealth. The second is that the liberal arts and pure sciences supply it. A defence of the first of these propositions will be postponed to the next chapter, since it arises in it most acute form when we try to give an account of the value of academic research. The defence of the second turns crucially upon matters of specific detail. Is it the case that all the subjects described as academic which have secured a place in the curriculum of the modern university are real sources of significant intellectual enrichment? They have (nearly) all had their detractors. Are social sciences, sciences? Is literary theory bogus? Is botany more than mere classification? Is theology a real subject? Is women's studies a genuine discipline? These are all serious and important questions which have exercised minds both within and without universities. Subjects come and go according to political, social and intellectual fashion. We may reasonably assume that impostors have sometimes joined the ranks of the intellectual, that the redundant can for a time go unnoticed, and that genuinely new subjects often have a struggle to establish their credentials. Differentiation between the many claimants to intellectual respectability requires a detailed examination of particulars that I do not propose to engage in here. It is enough for my purposes to make the assumption that many traditional academic subjects would survive such scrutiny. Even when they do, however, critical questions are not at an end. Of any such subject it may yet be asked — how is its value as a provider of intellectual wealth to be assessed?

The Professional and the Technical

Before turning to the question of assessment, there is a residual issue to be addressed. Following Newman I have drawn a distinction between liberal and technical/technological education. Where does this leave education in professions such as law, medicine and the church, all of which have figured in university study since its earliest days? The answer lies, I believe, in the recognition that legal, medical and theological education is radically incomplete if it remains at the level of the technical or even technological. Lawyers need to know how to prosecute cases successfully, doctors need to know how to cure people, and clergy must master the 'mechanics' of liturgy and sacrament. If these were all they came to know, however, there would be a serious deficiency in their training. But it is not enough that their practical skills are underwritten by more theoretical learning in the way that technology underwrites technique. Professionals also need an understanding of the significance of their profession. What is it to be an administrator of justice? In what do healers differ from witch-doctors? Why do we need priests and pastors? Without some consideration of these questions, the respective practitioners of these professions are mere functionaries, reduced to servers, and not formers, of social life. The profession of surgeon took some time to emerge from that of barber. Its emergence, it seems to me, had to do not merely with the mastery of different techniques, but with the acquiring of a certain self-consciousness. And this is where liberal education embellishes the technical and technological to create the professional. The idea and significance of law, the social role of healing, the metaphysical (and moral) meaning of liturgy and sacrament are necessary to the humanising, and one might say socializing, of these professions. Accordingly, jurisprudence figures in law degrees, medical ethics is (rightly) commanding an increasingly larger role in the education of doctors, and philosophical theology has always played a part in training for the priesthood. It is elements such as these which give professional training a place in university education of the 'liberal' kind, and such training forms an important bridge between the liberal and the technical. Even if it has not always been explicit, though it often has been, it is this self-consciousness that explains and justifies the traditional place such subjects have had in the curriculum of universities. They are, we might say, the place where the technical and the liberal meet because although their aim is practical mastery it is no less important, in the Socratic phrase, that they be able to give an account of themselves. This double nature means that professional subjects cannot be assessed as technical subjects can, and that no less than the arts and pure sciences, they raise issues about how the quality and success of a university education is to be judged. It is to this topic therefore that we now return.

Education and the Language of Commerce

Assessing the value of a technological education appears to have a relatively simple structure. Does it, literally, deliver the goods? In the last analysis, the point of technology is to solve practical problems, and though in any particular case it may be factually difficult to establish its success in doing so, conceptually the assessment of its success is a fairly simple matter. Technology does not set its own problems, except intermediately. Its ultimate problems are set for it by the social, commercial and industrial demands of the wider world in which it operates. It just is true that any technology can become outmoded — as the technology of gas lighting did — and at this point, whatever its intellectual interest, the technology has ceased to be of value. Its ceasing to be of value is not only marked, but established, by its failing in the market place. So, for instance, drugs that resulted from innovative research and have had huge success — Zantac (for ulcers) is a striking example — in their turn become no longer saleable, or, as in this case, have to find other, less prestigious outlets. Similarly students trained in a technology which becomes outmoded are no longer employable. With the advent of computer graphics the old skills and techniques of cartography are worthless. Typewriters and duplicators, hugely innovative and useful in their own day, are now quite without value. Home movies of the 16mm type have no place in the world of video cassettes.

It seems then that assessing the value of a technological education is a matter which the world at large will take care of. The same cannot be said of university education. How are we to know when it provides something of real value? There is an answer to the question 'how many computer programmers does society need?' — the answer is given 'when no more can find employment'. But to the question 'how many historians or philosophers or classicists does society need?', there is no such ready answer since people educated in these subjects can more readily be expected to find employment in personnel management or the civil service than as historians, philosophers or classicists. The question rather is what the study of philosophy, history, and so on, can contribute to human good. But how is this contribution to be assessed?

In recent times a marked and sustained effort has been made to address this question in a fashion which, as I shall argue, is inappropriate to its being adequately answered. One way of describing this effort is to say that academic value has been subjected to the language of commerce, the language, that is to say, of supply and demand. The idea is this: what better measure could there be than the demand for such courses? If university education is to be valued, this will be reflected in the demand for it. And allied to this thought is the idea that the success of individual courses can best be estimated by surveying the views of those who take them. To adopt this approach to academic value is to view the student as the buyer or customer of the offerings university teachers have to make. Such a change in view marks a highly significant alteration in the relationship between university student and university teacher. It is one which needs to be explored in detail. That it has come to be conceived in this way, it seems to me, is not in much doubt. The more important question is how it *ought* to be conceived.

The Student as Customer

The amalgamation of technological and academic institutions in a single system of higher education, together with an emphasis on increased participation and the continuing conception of tertiary education as essentially voluntary, has led to competition amongst institutions of higher education for students. One superficial consequence is the increasingly glamorous appearance of university prospectuses. Where formerly it was thought sufficient for these publications to inform, now they must attract and promote a suitably fashionable image. As a result, university prospectuses are much more sumptuous than they used to be.

This is, as I say, a superficial consequence, though nonetheless indicative of a change of attitude and perception. Two things need to be disentangled here. The first is that it is no longer sufficient, and ought never to have been, for university teachers to dish out to students whatever they choose to offer, or worse, whatever they can be bothered to. There was certainly a period, though quite a short one I think, in which arrogance and indolence played no small part in the attitude of university academics to teaching. Part of the cause of this was the radical divorce that government support for higher education had created between supply and demand. Thanks to statutory grants, automatic fees and generous support for capital projects, university teachers were protected from the mechanisms of account-ability that are such a marked feature of the market. This was always so in part, thanks to bursaries and benefactions, though at one time in Scottish universities students paid, literally, at the door of the lecture room, and the professor who could not attract or keep students felt this to his cost directly.

Given the amount of state money that went into university education it was inevitable, and wholly reasonable, that those who received it should, sooner or later, be called to account. And indeed accountability has become a watchword of higher education. There are many systems of 'staff appraisal' and 'academic audit' now in place which aim to institutionalise accountability. But something in the nature of market forces has also come to play a highly important part. The simple financial need for contemporary universities to attract, please and keep students is incontestable. There is not, as yet, a direct relation between this need and the prospering of particular classes and teachers, but a standard budgetary device, generally known as a Resource Allocation Model or RAM, is now very widely used, and has the effect of connecting the size, prosperity, and even continued existence of departments and subjects to the number of students they attract. In short, the student has become the customer.

Yet this is only the case if we focus on the supply side of the equation. Students are not customers in the evident sense that they do not part with their own money for the goods they receive. Though there are costs attaching to being a student which must be borne directly, the reduction of student grants, the introduction of loans and a flat-rate tuition fee having intensified these considerably, university education itself and the capital costs attaching to its provision remain largely free. This makes the conception of student as customer importantly partial. Students may vote with their feet, but they do not vote with their purses. They also vote with a near universal innovation — student course evaluation — opinion polls in short. There is much more to be said about these than would be appropriate in the present context. What is specially relevant here are some of the assumptions on which they are based.

Student Course Evaluation

The vast majority of universities now require their staff to issue questionnaires by means of which students may express their opinions of the courses of study they have taken. Opinion amongst academics differs as to the value of these, but it should be recorded that though the administrative burden of processing them tends to be mildly resented, they are resisted in principle by relatively few. Yet, as it seems to me, the assumptions on which these course evaluations rest are much more interesting and important than the mechanics of their deployment.

On what is a student to base his or her opinion of a course? The answer, I think, can only be subjective preference, not an estimation of objective worth. Why this is and why it matters are topics that take us to the heart of the confusions surrounding contemporary university education.

The provider of a consumer good has one main aim — to satisfy the pre-existent desire of the purchaser. Accordingly, the manufacturer of videos, the inventor of computer games, the restaurateur, the purveyor of holidays, must satisfy the desires of consumers. This is not to deny that consumer demand can be created, that consumers can be introduced to new forms of enjoyment. Still, if the desire to be satisfied is *mine*, I am sovereign in deciding what does and does not satisfy it. There are no doubt worthy and unworthy desires but it is not the business of the supplier to discriminate along these lines, except as a matter of personal restriction. Those who aim at successfully supplying the desires of the consumer can, for their own reasons, draw the line at being a pimp or a prostitute. Commercialism as such places no such restriction.

The point to focus on is the sovereignty of the consumer's desires and preferences. There is no place for producers setting out terms on which the goods they produce *ought* to be wanted or are *worth* wanting. Now the position is different where the relationship between giver and receiver is one between the expert and the inexpert. This is typically the case in education, but to see it most clearly we should first examine a case of non-academic education. One of the most valuable things that a modern teenager learns is the ability to drive. In the contemporary world, while being able to drive is not essential, it is nonetheless of enormous value, not just for personal convenience but for employment prospects as well. Interestingly, it is also the one instance of education that is governed almost entirely by market relations. The test of successful education in this case is not personal satisfaction with the manner or method of the instructor, but with a success as a result of his or her instruction. The good driving instructor knows what needs to be learned and how it is to be learned effectively. This is just what the pupil does not know, and hence the exchange is one between the expert and the inexpert. Though no doubt it is better, and may be more efficient, if the pupil enjoys the lessons, this is not the acid test.

Instruction in driving is illuminating, it seems to me, if we want to think clearly about the relation between teacher and pupil. It has these two important features, however. It is practical, and the measure of its success is a relatively straightforward test. Neither of these features is so evident in other more complex examples, and not evident at all perhaps in the case of university education. But we can go some way towards bridging the gap between driving and, say, English literature, by considering an intermediate case, namely learning a musical instrument.

The pupil who first comes to the piano has practical abilities to learn. However boring they may be, scales and finger exercises, and those rather mechanical 'studies' which many first-rate composers have devised, are an essential part of mastering the techniques without which great works of music cannot be played. But this technical mastery is only a foundation. The main business of the music teacher lies elsewhere, partly in the development of musicality and partly in a knowledge of which pieces of music are most worth playing. It is essential to the relationship between pupil and teacher, that the teacher knows what the pupil does not. Accordingly though (human beings being what they are) success will come more easily if pupils are quickly enabled to play the music they like, the purpose is to bring them to the point of playing music that is *worth* playing and being able to tell which music this is. It is at this point that they pass beyond the mere mastery of technique and are given a musical education. One way of putting this is to say that it is not merely the musical abilities but musical *taste* of pupils that must be educated.

The idea of educated taste is unfashionable. Yet its necessity in music, and the arts more generally, is undeniable. No good music teacher would take the preferences of the elementary pupil as sovereign; they await formation, and this is a major part of their musical education. Consequently, the test of a good teacher, and of a good course of instruction, is not that pupils are pleased, or have their pre-existent preferences satisfied, but that they become good musicians. To be inducted into the world of music is certainly to be inducted into a world of pleasure and enjoyment (though in my view it is not only this). But it is also a matter of being taught which pieces of music are most worth enjoying, and which it is best to take pleasure in. The crucial point to be observed is that the pupil/teacher relationship is one in which it is the knowledge and expertise of the teacher, not the pupil, which is sovereign.

Is there any reason not to say the same of academic subjects? Students for whatever reason decide to study, say, philosophy. But what philosophers are worth studying? By the nature of the case the novice student cannot say. I can, thanks to my own teachers, and my special aptitude for the subject. If this were not the case, why would I warrant the position of a recognized teacher of philosophy? It follows that the content of the curriculum and the conduct of courses are matters on which my opinion matters much more than the student's. It would be foolish as well as arrogant to deny that student questionnaires can be useful. Anyone may be unaware of defects that create obstacles to learning, and soliciting student opinion may reveal these. At the same time, to treat them like surveys of customer satisfaction is a profound error. A student, reasonably, may find Kant tedious and difficult, and find Edward de Bono more to their liking. Nevertheless, it is in Kant that far greater intellectual worth lies, which is not a judgement they are in a position to make, but one which they need to be taught how to make.

The anxiety which this line of thought, however cogent, gives rise to is that academics are once more given licence to teach whatever they like in whatever manner they like. The authority of the academic can be abused. In an effort to allay this anxiety, and to guard against those excesses and abuses of academic independence that have undoubtedly marred university education in the past, there has come into existence a system of peer review known as Teaching Quality Assessment. The merits and demerits of this are topics that any adequate account of university education must address. Before doing so, however, there is a further feature of recent university reform that needs to be considered, namely the modularization of courses. Important in its own right though this is, its examination is specially pertinent here since it has come about in large part because of the interest in meeting student demand, the same interest which has generated course evaluation.

Modularization

In the last few years very many universities have modularized their courses. The issue of greatest interest is whether this has, overall, been a good or a bad thing. But to address it, it is necessary first to say what modularization is and why it has come about. The first of these questions is easier to answer than the second.

Modularization is the breaking down of structured degree courses into distinct and separate components, which are then assembled by the student in accordance with rules of 'credit accumulation' such that at the end of a period of study the credits accumulated entitle the student to a degree. This system is one that has been in operation in the United States and elsewhere for a very long time. It facilitates what has been dubbed a 'cafeteria' system. Just as in a cafeteria, as opposed to a restaurant with a set menu, customers choose items from the dishes available in whatever combination or order they may prefer, so in a modular system the student puts together a course of study in which he or she has an interest. The change to modularization that has taken place in many British universities is still not quite the 'cafeteria' system that is typical of North America, but it nonetheless incorporates several important shifts. Formerly, it was exclusively dons who decided the combinations of subjects and the order of their study which were deemed to make most academic sense. Under the older system, which still prevails in certain places, students were largely told what to study and in which order to study it, though broadly speaking the Scottish degree had greater variety and flexibility within it than the traditional English degree. With modularization, it has become the students who decide these questions.

The considerations previously adduced about teachers and students and their relative expertise and inexpertness imply that there is reason to support a system of study structured by academics rather than by students. After all it is the academics who know and the students who have still to learn. Why then should such a change take place? The explanatory reasons are hard to uncover. University teachers undoubtedly felt under pressure to make the change, though why they felt this is obscure since there were no explicit central directives, or indeed any central body that could make them. Some were for the change, many against, but a sense of its inevitability seemed to grip the collective consciousness of the teachers in a large number of institutions. It is hard to say why this came about, but since our primary purpose here is to explore its rationale, the historical causes are ones on which we need not speculate. The rationale, fortunately, is easier to state. Student interest should dictate the choice of subject.

It is worth observing that though in a way British universities in this respect have come to ape North America, arguably the underlying motivation is significantly different. The American system, at least in the most important universities, was dictated by the interests of professors, not students. The modular system allowed teachers to offer courses specially tailored to their research interests and academic enthusiasms. It was then up to the student to combine these in ways which would add up to a cogent degree. This overstates the case a little. North American universities have always been subject to consumer demand in a way that British universities have not. As a result of a cultural belief in the value of liberal education and an accommodation between the competing interests of student and teacher, a system resulted in the US, and Canada, which could not be replicated exactly in the UK. The fact is history and tradition make a difference.

In the UK the modularization of courses was driven by the idea that the student is a customer whose requirements must be met. Flexibility was the watchword, but it may be questioned, in my view, just how important a belief in the desirability of flexibility was as a determining factor. What made the difference was anxiety about successful student recruitment. However this may be, the result is that the conception of student as customer has been substantially strengthened. It is not my purpose here to inveigh against modularization, even if there is reason to do so, but to observe that it has contributed substantially to the cogency of the language of commerce. University students are not only enabled, but encouraged, to pick and choose between the academic courses on offer as one chooses between the goods in a supermarket. The question is: Is this to their benefit? Or more precisely: is this to the benefit of their education?

It should be evident that the answer is that it is unlikely to be. The root of the word 'education' carries the meaning of being led, and this implies a subservient relation between those who are being educated and those who are educating them. Some educational theorists have set themselves to deny this. They speak of university education as though it were a matter of mutual exploration, and they do this partly under the inspiration of a certain kind of egalitarianism, which regards with suspicion *any* talk of superior and inferior, and with it any conception of elitism. This egalitarianism is misplaced, and still recognised to be so in many contexts. Surgeons do not, and are not expected, to regard their students as their medical equals.

Lawyers still trade upon special expertise. The same is true in sport and in music. The egalitarians suppose, I think, that claims to educational or intellectual superiority inevitably carry with them claims to moral, social or political superiority. Perhaps, in point of fact, they not infrequently do. This is a difficult matter to generalise about. But whatever unwarranted airs educational superiority may be inclined to give itself, it seems plain that teachers *ought* to be better at their subjects than pupils or students, or else their claims to be teachers are fraudulent. If education, at university or any other level, truly were a matter of mutual exploration between equal minds, why should some of those minds enjoy a salary and others not?

The fact is that university teachers either have superior knowledge and understanding to offer their students, or they have nothing. Student course evaluation may have its uses, and modularization may have brought advantages. It certainly seems that neither is likely to disappear in the immediate, or even intermediate, future. It is nevertheless the case that in large measure they both rely on and strengthen presuppositions about university education that, upon no very close examination, can be shown to be conceptually confused.

It would be misleading however to represent the present state of university education in Britain as though the conception of student as customer had carried all in its way. Despite the significant power shift which it has occasioned, it is still the case that within modules, and to a considerable extent within degree structures, the authority of the expert is the principal determinant. This autonomy in its turn is bolstered by the relative security of university teachers. Although tenure of position has been weakened in a number of ways, not least by changes in the law designed to end it, and though pseudo-commercial pressures have come to be felt as they have rarely been felt before, academics are still not subject to simple market forces in the way that the shopkeeper or the plumber is, and hence not really subject to the student as customer. For the most part their salaries are paid and their facilities provided by the public purse. This gives them a considerable measure of protection against the fluctuating fashions of student demand. Added to this is the fact that university teachers are not directly the employees of government bodies, as teachers in state schools are. The contemporary concern with accountability is such, however, this does not mean that within this protected sphere they are left alone to do as they think best. Alongside the 'checks' of course evaluation and student demand there has come into existence another form of scrutiny, namely peer review. Both university education and university research work are now regularly reviewed. The purpose of central, Funding Council sponsored peer review is to determine whether what the tax payer is paying for is being done properly. In this chapter it is the first that concerns us. The precise form this has taken, and ought to take, has been subject to change and dispute: first there was internal Academic Audit then external Teaching Quality Assessment, and finally external Quality Assurance of internal audit procedures.

Academic Audit

The term 'academic audit' itself signals something of the idea that has informed it, since it is an expression modelled on commercial practice. What it means, broadly speaking, is the introduction of systems of inspection which are designed to ensure that the courses on offer in a university all meet certain standards of acceptability. This way of stating it is slightly misleading. It has never been the case, except in rare and special cases, that individual academics or departments have been free to offer to students whatever they wanted to offer. Before academic audit all British universities (in contrast to some in America) had Boards of Studies, or some equivalent, whose approval had to be sought before new courses could be entered in the official list of educational provision. The awarding of degrees was subject to Boards of Examiners, usually including at least one external examiner from another institution. Normally these Boards were effectively committees of the Senate or Academic Council, the governing academic body of the university.

The novelty of academic audit lies rather in its making the system of approval much more formal and more uniform. The pursuit of uniformity has had two significant effects. The first is that academic audit does not concern itself directly with the intellectual *content* of courses, but with their form and presentation. The requirement is not that a course proposal should justify the intellectual worth of what it proposes to offer, but that it should meet general standards of a more abstract kind. Thus, courses have to set out clearly their educational aims and objectives, the ways in which these will be realised, the additional transferable skills they can be expected to secure for the students who take them, and the methods by which the attaining of these objectives is to be assessed. Generally, the effect of this attempt to 'audit' all courses uniformly has led to a high degree of abstraction because of the great variety of subjects to which it must be applied. In turn this has led to a somewhat superficial, and arguably fatuous, style of scrutiny. Thus a course in, say Harmony and Counterpoint, will meet the first of these requirements by stating that its objective is to teach students the elements of harmony and counterpoint. What else could its objective be? And is anything accomplished by requiring it to be formally stated? To the more telling question – is Harmony and Counterpoint worth teaching? – academic audit does not address itself.

There is reason for it not to do so. Academic freedom is to be prized greatly. Academic opinions tend to be held strongly. Standards of intellectual worth are themselves matters of genuine intellectual dispute. Consequently, to raise the deepest questions about intellectual worth is, usually, to open a hornets' nest, and one that very often admits of no practical resolution. Still, there are occasions on which it is just this question that needs to be asked. What matters about certain courses — sport science, postmodernist literary theory, creationist biology, peace studies, hotel management are plausible examples in my view — is whether they have the intellectual substance that warrants a place in a university. This is not to say that they do not, only that the question can reasonably be asked of them, unlike long-standing subjects such as physics, philosophy, pure mathematics, or political history.

The effect of academic audit as it has been introduced is to leave no place for such questions to be raised. Any subject, in fact, could meet its requirements. Courses in astrology could state aims and objectives, methods of study and transferable skills, and could be assessed according to how they achieved them. The gross intellectual defects of astrology would not be revealed in this way. If this is correct, it implies that the system of academic audit is seriously inadequate with respect to the purposes of universities, and, I think, any educational enterprise. A large part of the reason for this is that academic audit is built upon a commercial model. Assessment of efficiency and productivity can be as easily applied to candy floss as to computers. Efficiency and productivity say nothing about intrinsic worth.

The second effect of academic audit is a huge increase in the multiplication of bureaucracy. To prove this would require the assembly of substantial empirical evidence. Here I shall simply assert it, though I think the experience of most academics would lead them to concur. But at any rate, it is true that academic audit does not include any audit of itself. And yet any rational human activity should include some assessment of relative cost and benefit. What has, as yet, not been adequately addressed is this question: has the introduction of academic audit reduced the number of poor courses? As I have suggested, there is an interpretation of 'poor', i.e. intellectually lightweight, which the system by its nature cannot assess. But even if we restrict ourselves to the more superficial measure of effectiveness, there is still a question whether the introduction of academic audit has done enough in this respect to outweigh its undoubted costs. If my claim of hugely increased bureaucracy is correct, then these costs have been great, and it would be difficult to show, in my opinion, that the corresponding benefits, which are not negligible, have outweighed them.

However, I think it would be true to say that academic audit was not introduced in an entirely disinterested spirit. A large part of its motivation was the belief that external review by the Funding Councils was inevitable and that putting such systems in place, if it did not forestall it, would at least demonstrate a willingness to comply. Academic audit was in effect, the forerunner to Teaching Quality Assessment which was itself replaced by Quality Assurance.

Teaching Quality Assessment and its Successors

How are we to assess whether the teaching of a subject is being adequately done? This is a matter, let it be acknowledged, which it is wholly proper for the custodians of public finance to raise. The answer that the Higher Education Funding Councils came to initially was this: ask other teachers. In short, institute peer review. What needs to be questioned is not whether they have any right to raise this question, but whether this is the appropriate, and an effective, way to address it. In the face of the sort of system of teaching quality assessment that was employed through most of the 1990s and into the twenty-first century, the most important question to ask is whether *formal* institution of peer review is the right way to secure accountability. In my experience academics are almost obsessively self-critical as teachers. Long before TQA or QAA, there was constant review and assessment of teaching, motivated by the concerns of university teachers themselves. Even if it is unlikely to be believed by a sceptical reading public, the fact is that during my career as a university teacher (which started in 1975) there has never been a year in which I have not been involved in long, and often tedious, meetings whose sole purpose was to question the educational adequacy and intellectual relevance of courses on offer. This has been more true of undergraduate than postgraduate provision. Nevertheless, the image of the careless and indolent, not to say callous, academic which the popular images recorded in Chapter One so entertainingly describe, is generally at odds with the truth. Certainly it has *some* basis in fact, but at best it is a caricature and for the most part a figment of the imagination. There have indeed been indifferent and careless teachers in universities, throughout their long history no doubt. Yet in what occupation is something of the same not the case? Careless and indifferent doctors, worldly priests, unscrupulous lawyers, corrupt policemen, fraudulent businessmen, bullying teachers, self-serving politicians are the stock in trade of literature and the other arts since the time of Chaucer. But that the type, and the attitude, not merely occur, but are so prevalent in any given occupation that it needs instituted, systematic, central, assessment, is an inference requiring substantial additional justification. In the case of British universities in the last hundred years it is, as I believe, lacking.

However, lacking or not, the most important (and most telling) question to ask is whether, as it has been instituted, teaching quality assessment performs a real and valuable service which works to the educational interests of students. Investigation of this question, I think, is a matter of effect not ideas. The idea of inter-university peer review is interesting, and there is no reason in the abstract to object to the suggestion that expert teachers from one institution (or a number of institutions), should be asked to look critically at the educational provision of another. It all depends how it works.

How has it worked? No straightforward answer can be given to this question because 'it' has undergone almost continuous change over a decade. Teaching Quality Assessment (TQA) was replaced by Quality Assurance under the direction of a Quality Assurance Agency (QAA). Quality Assurance later collapsed partly under the weight of its own paperwork, partly because the results were so positive that they raised a doubt about its necessity, but chiefly because the system so manifestly failed to secure the support still less enthusiasm of universities. In its place came continuous Quality Enhancement (QE), the efficacy of which is yet to be determined.

Both TQA and QAA involved 'subject review', that is to say, the examination and comparison of teaching provisions for specific subjects on a nationwide basis. This system requires departments to submit a document describing what they do and offering a 'self-assessment'. The panel of reviewers than makes a short visit, of three days or so, during which classes are visited and staff, students and support staff are interviewed. There is an accompanying examination of prescribed documentation — reading lists, sample essays and exam scripts, student questionnaires etc. At the end of this process the assessing team is invited to award a rating on a large number of different aspects. These are summarised into a single grade that might be expressed linguistically — from unsatisfactory to excellent, say — or by a number — one to five in TQA, marks out of twenty-four in QAA. This grade is then made public, and was, as a matter of fact, used extensively in the construction by the media of university league tables.

Now the first point to be made about any system-wide method of assessment is that centralisation brings with it a large measure of standardisation. As in the case of academic audit this works against in-depth (and indeed accurate) assessment. Although there are shared educational objectives which can be stated in the abstract, in reality the degree of abstraction that is necessary obscures or ignores important differences between subjects and renders the application of these abstract criteria too remote to deliver meaningful and valuable judgements. How likely is it that, say, the teaching of building methods, biochemistry, and art history can be subject to the same criteria? Not very likely, reason suggests. If, in addition, the judgements are supposedly content-indifferent and aimed at assessing, not the intellectual worth of the subject matter, but the degree to which the 'objectives' that different subjects and departments have set themselves are achieved, the resulting overall judgement tells us very little indeed, next to nothing in fact.

A further point of some importance is that the final grade, since it is very coarse-grained, can, and has usually, disguised real areas of merit. Thus the existence of good and talented teachers can be overshadowed by poor teaching rooms, below average computing facilities and less than adequate career advisory services. It is not that these should not be criticized. Rather, the overall assessment, to those who do not read the details, leaves a mistaken impression with respect to many features of the institution in question. QAA tried to get around this by allocating sets of points – up to four in six different aspects of provision. But these were universally aggregated so that they could be expressed as a single result for the purposes of institutional comparison, thereby rendering the new system just as course grained as the old.

A third and perhaps most important point is that the emphasis on documentation led to a culture in which a paper trail was more important than the thing itself. In a few extreme cases, the required paper was invented; minutes of staff/student consultative committees that had never been held, for example. But in the majority of cases, where there was no attempt to 'cheat', the need to produce a paper trail meant that huge amounts of time were spent on doing so, with the ironic result that teaching was reduced in order to allow time to prepare for 'the QAA'. In short, the seemingly reasonable suggestion that universities be held accountable for the quality of their teaching rapidly led to a bureaucratic monster that was the enemy of time spent in the lecture hall and seminar room.

Finally (and this it was that finished off QAA) subject review revealed what might have been surmised anyway — that most university courses in Britain are conscientiously taught, and that though there is room for improvement no doubt, there is little point in persisting with a cumbersome and costly system of regular inspection. Accordingly, the next phase was ushered in — Quality Enhancement.

Quality Enhancement aims to incorporate some of the lessons learned from the systems that preceded it. First, it restores a large measure of importance to internal academic audit. Rather than review the educational provision of a given university in a given subject area, the idea of QE is to review the university's own system of review. Second, the system focuses on 'trouble-shooting'. That is to say, in recognition of the pointlessness of scrutinizing a perfectly good institution, QE makes a welcome assumption that all is well unless period review (every six years) suggests that it is not. However, ever fearful of complacency, and haunted by the spectre of those slackers and idlers with which Amis, Sharpe and Bradbury had such fun, QE introduces a new element — continuous enhancement — the perpetual improvement of courses and teaching.

We might call this the 'no standing still' conception of excellence. It denies what otherwise we might suppose to be true — that like other things, if well constructed and well taught, university courses can reach a standard beyond which no further improvement can reasonably be expected. Or to be more accurate: such further improvements as might be possible would not be worth the additional effort put into achieving them; that they are, in short, as good as they can be for all practical purposes. Now as it seems to me, the 'no standing still' conception of excellence flies in the face of experience. Sometimes things are as good as we are going to get them, and to recognize this is not a matter of complacency but of realism. In fact, *continuous* enhancement may not be a coherent ideal. If we have realistic standards of what can be achieved, then we should be able to achieve them, and to achieve them is to have done the best we can, in which case there is no scope for 'what is to be achieved' changing. Of course, we could reasonably look for further improvement if what is at issue is not educational attainment, but customer satisfaction, and it is striking that in introducing Quality Enhancement as a replacement for Quality Assurance, government ministers were quick to assert that student satisfaction would play an important part in its implementation. But this signals a shift from an educational to a consumerist conception of universities, something I have already discussed in the previous section on student course evaluation.

It seems, then, that the developing sequence of academic audit, TQA, QAA and Quality Enhancement has not yet reached a satisfactory resting place, and at least something of the cost, inefficiency and misconception of earlier phases remains in the latest. In order to appreciate the force of this conclusion it is important to stress that nothing has been said here against the idea of assessment as such. Nor is it claimed that the world of universities before TQA, QAA and so on was perfect. The point is rather that a huge amount of effort and a considerable sum of money has been spent on the introduction of formal systems of assessment, and that it is doubtful if all this has been well spent. The question is whether an unregulated system would be worse. To leave university teachers free to determine what is best for their students carries its risks, certainly. There will be carelessness, inefficiency and indifference. Such things will never be eliminated entirely. The only interesting question is whether academic audit and teaching quality assessment have reduced them to a degree that warrants the costs in time and money that they themselves have incurred. I think that a dispassionate approach to them will conclude that they have not.

The same issue, not necessarily with the same result, arises with respect to the other main function of universities — research. But before this issue can be considered directly, we need to ask whether and why universities should be involved in research at all.

CHAPTER 4

University Research

Teaching students is not the only purpose of the contemporary university. Even if Newman were right in the abstract that the sole (or at any rate principal) purpose of a university is to provide for the education of students, his reflections on the nature of a university would still be at some remove from contemporary reality. This is because today's university teachers are committed to, and convinced of, the importance of scientific and academic research. They regard this, not just as an adjunct or a spin off, but as an essential part of their function. Indeed, the Robbins Report declared the dual purpose of the transmission and extension of knowledge to be fundamental to a university, and this has not been seriously called into question.

Whether or not it was right to do so seems to me an essentially idle question, since this is how things are, and consequently it is a question I shall not inquire into. It has this further importance. Even if the arguments of the preceding chapter, which aimed to elicit something distinctive about university education are deemed to fail, a secondary claim can be that university teachers, unlike those in other institutions, have a duty to extend knowledge and not merely to transmit it. However, any claim for the importance of research in universities raises a second issue about justification. A university that educates students can at least call upon the respect and resources of the society in which it exists: university *education* benefits those who undergo it and thus enriches society more generally. What claim does university *research* have to public support? This question can seem specially pressing when applied to the more esoteric subjects that academics inquire into. It may be granted that research in pharmacology benefits us all, but why is it a good thing if, for example, someone somewhere discovers how the Abbey at Bury St Edmunds was run in the time of the Abbot Samson? And why is historical research of this sort more appropriate to a university, and in general more valuable, than studying railway timetables or calculating the frequency of winning numbers in the National Lottery?

Pure and Applied Science

To answer these questions we should start with natural science. The reason for doing so is this. Whereas people find it hard to see just why the public purse (or any purse, perhaps) should support the investigations of, for instance, Egyptology, the grammar of Middle High German, or the anthropology of the Trobriand Islands, most people imagine that scientific inquiry is a good thing. This, as I hope to show, is an indefensible prejudice, but it is nonetheless real. Thus it is important, for rhetorical purposes, to begin with the case of science, and if we can make a case for the value of research in pure science, and extend this to the arts and social studies we will have established the value of intellectual research in general.

There is a familiar and widely employed distinction in natural science (and in the discussion of its public funding) between pure (or basic) research and applied research. This distinction reflects, I think, a further, underlying, distinction between alternative explanations of the value of scientific inquiry, namely explanations by appeal to knowledge and to utility, an opposition which we have already encountered in the discussion of the value of universities in general. It is a distinction which needs to be examined more closely in the more specific context of scientific research.

According to this common way of thinking the value of pure or basic research lies in the furtherance of human knowledge for its own sake, whereas the value of applied research lies in its usefulness. There is no exclusiveness about this distinction, of course. Wherever we think the most cogent justification of science lies, we need not deny that basic research can turn up hypotheses that, in the future, prove to have been useful discoveries. James Clerk Maxwell's discovery of electromagnetism is a good example. It was not until some time after his death that radio waves were exploited for practical purposes. Conversely, applied research can add substantially to our knowledge. Galileo's invention of the telescope had huge consequences for astronomy. But the *aim* of pure and applied research is different. In the former the knowledge we hope to gain is sought for its own sake, while in the latter it is sought for a further end.

This, at least, is how the generally accepted picture goes. But it does not take very much reflection to see that, at best, familiar though this view of the matter is, it could only be part of the story. Consider first applied research. That its aim is utility is true. This, however, is a truth that tells us very little. 'Utility' is a more abstract concept than is often supposed and when we appeal to something's utility we have not in fact said anything substantial about its value, until, that is, we have answered the question — 'Utility to what end?'. Here, everyday speech is somewhat misleading. 'Useful', as it is commonly meant, is a positively charged word; it is conversationally taken to mean 'useful for some good purpose'. Logically, however, a discovery is useful if it serves *any* purpose, good or otherwise. When people commend applied research they normally have in mind research which results in, for example, improved ways of promoting health, producing food, increasing the efficiency of transport or reducing the cost of communications. In short, the utility of applied research is tacitly associated with additions to the sum of human welfare (though we have no reason to restrict it to exclusively *human* welfare; utility explains the value of veterinary science). This tacit assumption closes the gap between utility and value because welfare is readily intelligible and widely accepted as a suitable goal both for scientific inquiry and for public support, the sort of goal, moreover, which is generally thought to require no further justification.

Whether it does or not, whether, that is to say, an increase in welfare always justifies the thing that produces it is a question to which we shall have to return. For the moment the main point is to observe that the utility of applied research explains its value only and in so far as it is utility for some *good* end and not merely for some end. Applied research, in short, can be useful without by that fact alone being justified, because its usefulness may as easily be to harmful as to beneficial ends. Those who take a dim view of the arms industry would not deny that scientific research can develop better weapons, but they would deny that such research is for the general good.

Knowledge for its Own Sake

This contention about the normative emptiness of 'utility' is not a novel or even very surprising conclusion, but it has an implication other than that which it is sometimes believed to have. It is often thought that defending scientific inquiry on the basis of its usefulness is selling it short, because utility is an instrumental, not an intrinsic, value. The appeal to utility does not really explain the value of science *as such*, but only of the value of the *consequences* scientific knowledge and inquiry may have. If true, this suggests that an adequate explanation of the value of science must locate the value in science *itself*. It is at this point that knowledge as opposed to utility enters the argument, because the further value to which any adequate justification of science must point is normally thought to be knowledge for its own sake.

The value of knowledge in and for itself is a point upon which Newman's argument in *The Idea of a University* turns. His defence is of 'knowledge as its own end'. Now although nothing said so far conflicts with Newman's contention, the claim that knowledge *in itself* is valuable is one which we need reason to make. Otherwise, it amounts to no more than a slogan. To accept that utility is not a complete explanation of the value of research, even where utility is in fact served, is to agree that there must be some other value involved which makes it usefulness to a good end. But what this value (or range of values) actually *is*, is a further issue. It can certainly be welfare, as the conversational implication of 'useful' generally assumes it to be, understanding welfare to mean, broadly, health , happiness and prosperity. What the argument of the last section shows is this: we can mount a satisfactory explanation of the value of applied research, even if welfare is the only value that utility serves. However, while such an explanation does attribute value to the acquisition of knowledge as a means, it makes no appeal to its intrinsic value.

Now it follows from this that to demonstrate the insufficiency of pure utility, is *not* to show that the pursuit of knowledge for its own sake must enter the discussion. The promotion of welfare, human or animal, is an end logically sufficient for a complete explanation of its value. For all that has been said so far, it may be the only one. Why do we need to add knowledge to the calculation? It is all very well to *assert* the value of 'knowledge as its own end' or to *declare* 'pure' research more fundamental to the scientific enterprise. But anyone persuaded that utility to the end of welfare is the best explanation of the value of research is at liberty to argue that, since *only* the value of applied research could be explained in this way, the pursuit of pure or basic science which has no connection with application cannot be lent any special value or importance — except perhaps in terms of the personal curiosity of the scientist, and the argument about the insufficiency of utility does nothing to counteract this contention.

The Value of Knowledge

Such a claim is one which popular opinion finds attractive. Moreover, it especially appeals to those responsible for the public financing of scientific research, precisely because of the ease with which an explanation in terms of general welfare can command public support. If scientific research can be shown to contribute to an increase in the well-being of society as a whole, expenditure upon it is easy to defend. Scientists themselves are sometimes led to concur with this line of thought just because they acknowledge the same pressure for the sort of political justification which will win credibility in the competition for limited resources. Usually, however, whatever they may say by way of public defence of their work, personally they remain convinced of the importance of basic research. It is just that they do not know how to make this personal conviction publicly persuasive. Yet by harnessing the justification of pure research to that of applied research, they are making a concession that strikes many people, and not just scientists, as defective.

If the explanation of the value of pure research is that it will, eventually, through technical application, promote the goal of welfare, this has two implications, and neither of them seems satisfactory. First, it makes pure research secondary to applied research,. This appears to be contrary to the essential character of science as an independent human endeavour, one of very ancient lineage indeed. Since the time of the ancient Greeks, knowledge of the natural world has been pursued for its own sake. Secondly, it implicitly admits that if we were ever to know, or at least be reasonably sure, that some piece of research would *not* lead to technological innovation, we could attribute no objective, socially defensible value to it. To put applicability at the heart of the defence of research is thus to declare that research which is useless (from the point of view of welfare) is valueless. We have already seen reason to doubt any identification of the valuable with the useful. The case against doing so may now be strengthened by the observation that a great deal of research in physics, astronomy and biology (where we find theories commonly regarded as being amongst the greatest scientific discoveries — those of Copernicus, Newton, Darwin and Einstein for instance), has no known practical application. This seems an odd and unfortunate implication.

Its odd and unfortunate character, however, does not render it false. A thoroughgoing utilitarian, concerned solely with public welfare, as many public policy makers are, can consistently maintain that only research that can be shown actually or with a reasonable probability to contribute usefully to welfare can be said to have value. (Those who are drawn to utilitarianism as a basis for social policy rather than a general approach to evaluation might restrict their conclusion to the claim that *public* expenditure can only be justified on useful science. Private donors can do as they wish, in accordance with their interests.) But even if this contention can be held consistently, it is one that scientists and many others feel strongly inclined to reject. They do so because intuitive conviction tells them that something essential is missing.

'Intuitive conviction' is sometimes a politer name for prejudice, of course, so whether this intuitive conviction is rationally defensible or not must be a legitimate subject for further discussion. This is the point of wondering if 'knowledge its own end' is anything more than a slogan. Nevertheless it is in the context of this further discussion that appeals to knowledge for its own sake are most often made. The scientific utilitarian's error, it is alleged, is to conflate the useful with the valuable (which we have already seen to be a mistake) and hence to ignore the value of knowledge for its own sake (which has yet to be shown). Now this response, which we have reason to think would be Newman's, is only half right, it seems to me. I have argued that it is indeed erroneous to suppose that nothing other than the useful is valuable, where by 'useful' we mean 'that which promotes welfare'. But it is equally mistaken to suppose that knowledge is always valuable. This is because it is easy to show that there can be genuine knowledge which is wholly worthless.

It is not hard to think of examples. There is a fact of the matter as to how many people listed in a telephone directory between, say, pages 171 and 294 have surnames beginning with the same letter as the street in which they live, and quite some time could be spent ascertaining this fact. But the knowledge that we came to possess as a result of doing so would be quite worthless and the time spent in gaining it completely wasted. This is because the knowledge we would acquire is not worth having. Nor is this a matter of the relatively pedestrian character of the inquiry. Suppose, to take another example, I am cutting grass. There is a fact of the matter as to how many blades of grass I cut in the space of five minutes and whether the rate at which I cut it falls in some regular proportion as the length of time I spend at the task increases. This is not a case for simple counting, and we can imagine sophisticated mathematical methods by which I might try to ascertain these facts. But the sophistication of the methods does not make the knowledge of these facts worth possessing. As this example shows, there can be worthless knowledge that only someone possessing considerable skill and displaying methodological imagination can arrive at; but it is still worthless.

If it is easy to think of such examples, however, it is equally easy to amend them in ways that give the worthless knowledge some value. Take the first example of the telephone directory. Imagine that an eccentric millionaire has established a large cash prize for the first person to come up with the answer. The knowledge that was formerly worthless has now become worth obtaining, if I obtain it quickly enough, and the use of my time in doing so has become a plausible investment of effort. Or, to take the second case, I may be engaged in some sort of cost-benefit analysis, aimed at helping me decide whether I would not be better to employ a gardener than to do the work myself. In this case the knowledge I seek is not worthless but is, rather, information required for rational decision making.

These two emendations present slightly different cases. In the first, the connection between the knowledge and the value of knowing it is a wholly fortuitous one. It happens that this detail about the telephone directory is worth knowing because someone has whimsically made it so — any other randomly chosen fact might have served as well. In the second, there is a more internal connection; the knowledge is required by the particular decision in hand — an accurate cost-benefit analysis of my efforts at gardening requires knowledge about those efforts and not about any other randomly chosen fact. In both emendations, knowledge that was hitherto valueless is given a value, by being put in a context. But in the second example the context lends significance to the knowledge in a less than wholly fortuitous way. It explains why *that* item of knowledge, as opposed to any other, was required.

This is a difference of some importance, and I shall return to it. But before doing so, for present purposes there is a feature of both examples that is worth noting. I have argued that the appeal to knowledge for its own sake as a justification of scientific endeavour is unsatisfactory because there is knowledge that is quite valueless. Any piece of valueless knowledge, however, may become valuable if we place it in an appropriate context. Thus the distinction between valueless and valuable knowledge is a distinction between contextless knowing and knowing within the context of some further purpose. In the examples given this further purpose turns out upon inquiry to be connected with welfare. In the first it is crudely so — monetary benefit — and in the second less crudely but no less obviously so — the minimization of wasted effort. What this shows is that where a resulting increase in knowledge is inadequate as a justification of research, the remedying of this inadequacy is most easily accomplished by a further appeal to welfare. But if so, we are back where we began; the appeal to knowledge has not allowed us escape from the primacy of applied research or the overriding end of welfare promotion.

This is true only of these examples, of course. What they demonstrate is not the pre-eminent value of welfare, but that valuable knowledge requires a context in which it is sought. The examples chosen also show that this context may indeed be the promotion of welfare. But it need not be. We can readily think of other contexts that will do as well. Take for example, the pursuit of pleasure. Train spotters and cricket buffs accumulate large quantities of otherwise trivial and worthless fact in the pursuit of a hobby they enjoy. Taken in isolation what they know is of little significance, but they derive pleasure from the fact of knowing it, however odd this may seem to those who do not share their enthusiasms. Engaging in a hobby provides a relevant context in which knowledge comes to have value.

This sort of example may not be thought to advance the argument much. Should we not regard the pursuit of pleasure as an aspect of the promotion of welfare? I do not think that we should, because people can and frequently do pursue pleasure at the expense of their own welfare — the pleasure of drugs or sex, for example, may jeopardise their health or happiness. Persistent drug taking is most easily explained by the pursuit of pleasure over the promotion of health and well-being. However, I do not propose to argue this particular case in detail here. The very possibility of making a distinction between pleasure and welfare shows that attributing value to the acquisition of knowledge by locating it in the context of promoting welfare only proves that *some* such context is needed; it does not follow that welfare promotion is the only one. And if the pursuit of pleasure is not regarded as a convincingly distinct context, others are easily thought of. The administration of justice, for instance, is one such non-welfare alternative. "Where was so-and-so on the night of the such-and-such?" is, in itself, a question of idle curiosity. It is transformed into a matter of consequence when the context in which it is asked is one concerned with punishing guilt and protecting innocence.

The argument so far has shown this, then. The distinction between pure and applied scientific research suggests that we should seek different explanations of their value. It is a common and tempting thought that while applied research is justified by its usefulness, the justification of pure scientific inquiry lies in the contribution it makes to human knowledge. But however tempting this thought may be, it is deficient in both particulars. On the one hand the utility of a discovery is not an adequate explanation of its value until we know what purpose its utility serves; research may be as useful to a bad as to a good end. On the other hand, since there can be genuine knowledge that is nonetheless trivial, the mere acquisition of knowledge is not an achievement unless it serves some larger purpose. What we have seen is that this larger purpose need not be the promotion of welfare, even if in the case of applied science it often is. There are other purposes which provide a context for knowledge that would otherwise be valueless. It is in these contexts that it takes on a value. The question now arises as to whether there is some such purpose which science in itself peculiarly serves and within which the knowledge its inquiries produces is lent value.

Knowledge and Understanding

There seems to me an obvious answer to this question, and one which I propose to explore and defend. This is the suggestion that pure science is not the acquisition of *knowledge* for its own sake, but rather the pursuit of *understanding*, within which the acquisition of knowledge has a central part to play.

It is not altogether easy to know how to defend the claim that understanding is valuable for its own sake. Here it will be useful to consider further the question I promised to return to, namely whether welfare can be considered valuable in its own right. This is because the same sort of difficulty arises for welfare as for understanding; it is a value so basic that it is difficult to establish a firmer ground upon which we might secure its justification.

At this point we can profitably turn, I think, to ancient classical ideas. Let us mean by welfare something like Aristotle's concept of *eudaemonia* or human flourishing. Within the Aristotelian scheme of thinking, human beings, like plants and other animals, have a nature which can flourish or be stunted, and the nature of a thing determines what its flourishing will consist in. So, just as some plants thrive where it is hot and dry, others thrive only where it is wet and cold. It is in this sense that we can speak of a plant's welfare and the conditions that help or hinder it. So too with animals, and with human beings. Poor diet, poor health, poor living conditions and poor human relationships prevent human beings from developing the potential that their natural aptitudes and capacities make possible. Human beings deprived of certain conditions end up physically and psychologically stunted. Conversely good diet, health and so on, allow them to flourish as human beings and can thus be regarded as important aspects of their welfare which there is reason to promote.

Aristotle's notion of *eudaemonia* has rather broader connotations than the modern concept of welfare that is its most obvious contemporary counterpart, and often its literal translation in fact. For us, welfare is primarily a matter of material, and to a lesser extent psychological, flourishing. To the modern mind health and prosperity are most readily thought of as constituent elements of welfare, though personal happiness (or psychological adjustment) is generally included as well. But Aristotle takes a fuller picture of human nature. He means to encompass the intellectual and the artistic no less than the material and the psychological. For Aristotle, a person whose mind is unextended and who has no artistic sensibility is no less stunted than someone who is physically disabled or psychologically disordered. We need not argue about the respective adequacy of these two conceptions, however, for there is no matter of real contention here. Even if we restrict the concept of welfare to the material and the psychological, as common contemporary usage does, we can allow that human beings have other aspects to their nature besides these — the life of the mind and of creative endeavour being obvious candidates. Once this truth is accepted, it follows that these other aspects of human nature also have their flourishing, or perhaps it would be best to say, in these respects too we can plausibly speak of excellences and ideals.

Aristotle himself gives the exercise of intelligence a central role in the development of a fully rounded human life, though there is some uncertainty amongst scholars over the interpretation of his thinking as to its precise role. Still, he distinguishes a number of different ways in which human intelligence may exhibit itself and for most of the *Nicomachean Ethics,* the central work in his exposition of these ideas, *phronesis* or practical intelligence seems to be the mental faculty which binds human virtues into a unity. At the end of this work (which probably consists in notes on rather than the text of his lectures), it seems to be *theoria,* a more contemplative intelligence akin to pure intellectual inquiry, that is given pride of place as the crowning achievement of the life of the mind. We do not have to resolve this interpretative tension here, however. It is sufficient for present purposes to note the following implications of this Aristotelian way of thinking. First, even if we make welfare or happiness (in the more narrow modern sense) the supreme value, we thereby automatically attribute value to understanding. This is because we can only realize welfare in so far as we understand the nature of the things whose welfare it is. To fail to understand their nature is to be rendered incapable of promoting their good. We need to *know* about plants, for instance, in order to *make* them thrive. The goal of intelligence, therefore, is understanding. Secondly, though understanding has a crucial role to play in the promotion of welfare, it can also be found in forms independent of it. The mind can exercise itself in ways that do not contribute to material or psychological well-being. If such exercises are to be valued the reason cannot therefore lie in such a contribution. Where then does it lie?

The Value of Understanding

In answering this question it should first be repeated and emphasized that the life of the mind is as much a part of the nature of human beings as the life of the body or the emotions and *a priori,* that is, without illicit presupposition, there is consequently just as much reason to value the full development of mind as of body or personality. To restrict the development of mind to its activity in the service of welfare seems a quite arbitrary limitation, consequently. Of course it is true that in endeavouring to arrive at and improve our understanding of the content and promotion of welfare we do indeed require extensive and sophisticated mental processes; modern technology (something to which we will return) is perhaps the most impressive demonstration of the extent to which practical reasoning is able not only to satisfy recurring human ends but also to widen human horizons about how those ends might be extended and integrated. The marvels of information technology are a good demonstration of this.

Still, impressive though the development of technology has been, the almost equally long-standing human project of understanding both the natural and the social world to the end not of increasing welfare but of reducing ignorance, confusion and misconception, is no less impressive an outcome of intellectual analysis, reflection and inquiry. It is in connection with this second project that we find a context in which research that has no practical application, which is useless in the normal, everyday sense, may nevertheless have value, a context, that is to say, in which the acquisition of knowledge takes on the right sort of significance. If we take the promotion of welfare to be a justifiable end for human endeavour, on the grounds that welfare is to be understood as nothing other than a central part of human flourishing, we can equally well argue for the promotion of understanding, on the grounds that it too is an aspect of human flourishing. A concern with welfare is a concern to ameliorate the human condition from the point of view of suffering and hardship; a concern with understanding is a parallel concern to ameliorate the human condition from the point of view of ignorance and misunderstanding.

This could hardly be said to be a dramatic conclusion. Nor is it meant to be. Despite all the (necessary) effort that has been put into arriving at it, it is rather mundane. The point, however, has been to arrive at it as the result of an argument which, I think, has the following important feature. In public discussions of the respective value of science and technology, the defence of applied research is generally taken to be easy and the defence of pure research more difficult. This is because the connection between applied research and welfare is presupposed and its justificatory adequacy assumed, and because claims on behalf of knowledge for its own sake have a less than convincing ring. But once we ask for the ground upon which welfare is to be valued, we arrive at an explanation in terms of human flourishing from which a precisely parallel defence of the value of understanding may be mounted. The point to emphasise in this way of thinking is not so much the conclusion that understanding is to be valued, but that its value is to be explained, or perhaps more accurately, clarified, in just the same way that the value of welfare is. This means that, contrary to common opinion, appeals to welfare enjoy no advantages over appeals to understanding and for this reason the

defence of pure inquiry need not be made subservient to the defence
of applied research.

The Useful and the Enriching

There is, perhaps, some point in reiterating here conclusions that
were drawn in Chapter Two. The argument of this chapter, which
purports to show that increases in understanding for its own sake
are to be valued no less than increases in economic prosperity, is
sometimes thought less than convincing because of a tendency to
confuse the concepts of prosperity and enrichment, concepts closely
allied to those of purchasing power and wealth creation. Some of the
points that were made in Chapter Two are worth repeating. Let us
agree that applied research is valuable because it increases prosperity, at least potentially, and that prosperity is a universally recognized good. People are inclined to think of prosperity in terms of
material resources, and in many instances this is no doubt correct.
Yet it is not hard to see that the value of some material resources lies
in the further goods they are able to secure. For example, while an
increase in the supply and variety of food may be a straightforward
material benefit, improvements in methods of transport more often
take their value from the existence of valuable places to go. Better
roads and bridges are to be valued in large part because of the holiday resorts, sports centres, concert halls and so on that they enable
us to travel to. On their own, in fact, they have very limited value. In
this way, the value of such material benefits can often be seen to
derive from the value of a non-material benefit, the composition and
performance of music, for instance. To suppose otherwise is like
supposing that the value of books lies primarily, not in their being
items for intellectual appropriation, but in the fact that they generate
employment in paper production and printing. The truth is the
reverse; paper production and printing take their value from the
interest that lies in books, magazines and newspapers.

Conversely, not all increases in strictly material prosperity can
reasonably be regarded as real benefits, because here, as elsewhere,
the law of diminishing marginal utility applies. The application of
food science to produce a second flavour of potato crisp may be said
to be the provision of a benefit, while its application to produce a
thirty-second flavour can hardly be. The same can be said of more
significant cases. The development of a drug for the alleviation of a
serious illness is a great benefit; the development of a second drug

whose sole advantage is marginally reduced side effects is much less obviously so.

It follows from both these considerations that increasing the material resources of a society is not the same as enriching it, and that the enrichment of society not only allows but requires the promotion of non-material ends. Scientific research, even if it serves no other end than the enhancement of human understanding, may therefore, along with art, sport and entertainment, play as important a part in the enrichment of human life as does more 'practical' or utilitarian inquiry. More importantly, perhaps, it does so in an integral way. Whereas the justification of applied research requires reference to a further end before its utility can be said to be truly valuable, understanding enriches the life of the mind directly. The mind flourishes, we might say, in so far as it understands, and academic research is to be valued, therefore, in so far as it contributes to this understanding.

Research Assessment

Though the relevant facts may be hard to amass, conceptually speaking the utilitarian assessment of applied research is relatively easy. Does it increase the stock of human welfare or not? The answer lies very largely in the satisfaction of consumer demand. But what about the pure research of scholars and scientists? The question here is whether human understanding has been increased and this is very much more difficult. How is it to be assessed? How are we to know whether the researches in which universities engage are genuine additions to human understanding? On the assumption that there is no real role for demand here, an assumption which we will consider a little later, the answer which has been arrived at by the University Funding Councils is "Research Assessment". As with Teaching Quality Assessment, Research Assessment is a system of peer review, and a proper estimation of its value, in my view, also turns on how it works in practice. As far as the *idea* of Research Assessment is concerned there can hardly be an objection to exercises in which those who claim to be advancing human understanding with respect to some subject are required to convince the experts in that subject that an advance has indeed been made. There can hardly be any objection because this is precisely what happens anyway with submissions to academic journals and publishing houses. If I wish to have an essay enter the currency of the journals, I need to convince an expert editor that it is intellectually worthy enough to appear there. This is a parallel which we will find reason to consider further.

In short, although the term 'research assessment' is relatively recent, the practice is probably as old as academic publishing. What is new is the introduction of one-off, standard, across the board, national assessment exercises for the purposes of distributing financial resources in support of academic research. What is most worth examining, therefore, is the *institutionalization* of research assessment in this form. Whether it is a good idea is not the main question therefore, but whether it really has secured greater accountability in this area of public expenditure, and ensured better value for money. This is, in the end, its purpose and sole rationale.

There have now been several such exercises and their results have had important consequences for the distribution of finance. However this is not our direct concern. To examine the merits of the system it should first be explained how it works. The rules have varied between different exercises, but the basic method is the same. Universities are required to list those members of staff who are 'research active'. Research activity is understood in terms of successful publication. For each member of the research active staff a quantity of published material is submitted. This work is then subjected to the critical scrutiny of a panel of expert judges. The judges are required to decide how far the work submitted matches up to standards of national and international 'standing'. Depending on the proportion of staff for each subject in each institution meeting these standards, a grade is awarded. It is upon this grade that the Funding Councils decide the level of financial support that is to be given to academic research in the institutions under review in proportion to the number of research active staff.

There is no doubt that universities have taken these Research Assessment Exercises (RAEs) very seriously. The recruitment and rewarding of staff and the allocation of resources within universities have all been heavily influenced by the desire for improved RAE ratings. And there is indeed good reason for them to do so, since the measure of a university's success in terms of RAE grades has very largely determined its academic standing within the university system as a whole. Just which is cause and which is effect is difficult to assess here, however. It may be that RAE ratings are taken at face value, and intellectual status accorded in line with them. Alternatively, it may be that there is a sort of circularity. Just as on the stock market a firm's share price can rise not so much because its balance sheet makes investors believe it is doing well, but because investors believe that its balance sheet will make *others* believe it is doing well, so it may be that particular departments come to be held in high regard because everyone believes that everyone else believes that their high RAE rating will lead to this result.

If it is this second more complex relationship between RAE rating and academic standing which truly prevails, there is a danger that institutionalized RAE has the nature of a race in which no one believes, but in which everyone has reason to take part, and to do so vigorously and with the appearance of enthusiasm. This makes it all the more important, in my view, to attempt as impartial an examination as possible of its merits and demerits. To do so we need to look first at its procedures and then at its consequences.

One thing to be said about RAE is that it is a snapshot procedure. The quality of research is assessed according to the staff in post at a certain date. For instance, one such RAE took as its basis selected publications of academic staff in post on the 31st March of the year in which the exercise took place. Now this permitted the following. Universities were able to recruit staff (with publications) very shortly before this date, while the same staff, having been given flexible contracts, were able to leave not long after, in some cases even before the results of the assessment had been announced. This had the consequence that the RAE grade awarded was in part based upon work done elsewhere by people who only fleetingly belonged to the institution in question. In short, the published grade included an estimation of people and publications that had very little to do with the institution whose grade it was. Of course, something of this sort is possible with any snapshot procedure, and perhaps it is impossible to avoid. The point of drawing attention to it, however, is to try to arrive at a true estimation of RAE — just what does it tell us about the institutions that are assessed?

A second procedural point is this. In an effort to avoid crude estimation of worth in terms of mere *quantity*, RAEs have come to rely upon judgements of *quality* by the assessing panels. Together with division of labour within panels, necessitated by the formidable size of the task, this has meant that the grade awarded to any given institution for any given subject has not infrequently rested heavily (though never, as far as I know, exclusively) on the judgement of a single individual. Now as the editor of any academic journal knows, there can be radical differences of genuinely held opinion between equally well qualified referees over the intellectual worth of material submitted for publication. These differences continue after publication of course — poor reviews are evidence of this possibility. And they may be expected to persist when the published material is used for the purposes of RAE. It follows that, while the desire to avoid an abject worship of quantity is commendable, reliance upon judgements of quality must give special authority to the opinions of some over others when there is good reason not to do so. The resulting system, in fact, is one in which academic worth is identified with *opinions about* worth. To see the error in this, consider again the case of academic journals. When an article is submitted, the editor, with the assistance of referees, must form a judgement about the worth of the piece, and on the strength of this judgement accept it or reject it. But though there can be good judges and bad, the opinion of even the best does not *determine* that an essay accepted for publication is intellectually substantial or important. Whether it is or not, is determined by its reception and influence in the wider world and the longer term.

If this is correct it follows that a proper process of research assessment would not consider the *content* of published work, but the *effect* of its publication on the subject to which it is a contribution. The trouble is that though there are some very clear cases in which this can be done — who could seriously deny that Darwin, Mendel, Einstein, Fleming, Namier, Leavis or Wittgenstein were major contributors to the growth of human understanding — to do so on a systematic regular nation-wide basis introduces a range of intangibles and imponderables that would render any clear outcome impossible.

An illustration of the difficulty involved in doing this is to be found in the use of citation indices, which have been deployed for this purpose mostly in the United States, but in other places also. Citation indices record the number of times a book or published paper is referred to by other writers. The problem is that the counting of citations is indiscriminate. That is to say, it does not register the reasons for or the source of the citation. Consequently, a paper which is cited largely for the errors and misunderstandings it contains will appear as readily as one that is commended, and individuals and groups can inflate their appearance in the index by citing their own work. In principle these problems can be circumvented, but in practice the task of producing a count of 'quality' citations is almost impossible. In any case, there is the question of time-scale. A work that causes an immediate stir may, after a time, come to be regarded as of little lasting significance. Conversely, it may be some years before the value of truly pioneering research is recognized. An even greater difficulty is this. Some highly influential intellectual work gets rapidly absorbed into its subject. This is especially true where its influence is chiefly on methods of study rather than by its results or conclusions. A good example of this is to be found in my own subject, philosophy. J.L. Austin, who taught in Oxford in the 1950's, published relatively little, but his influence over many years on how philosophy was studied — the so-called ordinary language method — was immense. I doubt if any citation index would reveal the extent of this influence because most of the papers and books that adopted his method did not expressly acknowledge the fact. Finally, there is the phenomenon of the unpublished contribution to scholarship and scientific inquiry. Intellectual exchange is not limited to the printed page. Academics meet in conferences, special seminars, visitor programmes and the like. The important contributions that may be made to a subject on such occasions sometimes show up in footnotes and acknowledgements. More often, I would guess, they do not. Any measure of intellectual worth which does not capture these, omits a highly significant factor in the growth and development of human understanding and, of course, measures that focus exclusively on publication or the citation of publication will not do so. To arrive at an accurate assessment of research we need to go beyond the printed page.

This is something that more recent versions of the RAE have tried to do. In addition to published items assessed in terms of quality, Units of Assessment (UoAs) have been invited to supply quantitative information on research student numbers, research grants awarded, and the like. These have only counted as additional factors that may tip the balance where the judgement on published material is uncertain. Now so many factors influence postgraduate students in the choice of where to study that it is difficult to see that any statistic of this sort could reveal much about the quality of research being undertaken, though the position is in some places that postgraduate student numbers have been expanded at the expense of standards. But the appeal to success in research grant application as a mark of excellence is different since these are usually awarded on a competitive basis. This raises the question, though, whether, given the doubts and difficulties I have raised about direct qualitative judgement, successful research grant application might not be a *better* standard, rather than just an additional indicator. It is a topic I shall take up in a later section. For the moment, though, it is worth noting that figures on research students and research grants are referred to in the jargon of the RAE as 'minor volume indicators'. This in itself is significant, because it reflects an often unspoken assumption — that academic achievement is properly regarded as a kind of production.

The Language of Production

RAEs employ the concept of the 'research active' academic. This has been identified almost entirely with the concept of those who are 'productive' and in turn this is measured in terms of 'output', which is to say published books and papers. Nor is it uncommon for university reports to speak of their aims and purposes in terms of 'deliverables'. This is the natural language of industry, not of academia, of course, but its use has become widespread and its employment has a number of important consequences.

First, any system of assessment which places exclusive emphasis on published 'output' has no place for according merit to individuals who are truly masters of their subject but who do not commit their thoughts to print, or do so only rarely. Academics who keep abreast of their subject, who are truly expert, and who are well placed, sometimes uniquely so, not only to teach undergraduates but, through the supervision of postgraduate research, to contribute to the advancement of their subject, cannot, by the nature of the case, figure in such assessments. This has a double defect. First, if we really are concerned with whether public (or other) funds are being well used, we ought to know about such people, and a focus upon published output will not tell us. Secondly, a heavy or even exclusive emphasis on publication easily works against the judgement of the truly expert. Someone who is thoroughly versed in a subject may judge, with good reason, that the prospects of contributing something really novel to it are small and likely to be realized only occasionally. Professional judgement in these circumstances dictates that worthwhile publication will be relatively rare. A constant pressure to publish works against this better judgement.

The declared intention of RAEs to assess research in terms of quality rather than quantity is a commendable attempt to resist this pressure. But the pressure comes from several sources and not just official Research Assessment Exercises. One of these is individual career prospects. 'Publish or perish' has been a familiar maxim in the United States for some considerable time and has come to figure in

British university life to a degree that was never previously the case. There are exceptions of course, but by and large, it is no longer enough for a British academic to be a good scholar, a conscientious teacher and an efficient administrator in order to secure promotion and advancement. It is also necessary to have published reasonably extensively. I have no doubt that this has come about in part as a reaction to an earlier condition in which universities were more or less a law unto themselves, where relatively little was demanded in the way of accountability and where, accordingly laziness and carelessness were unduly protected. Just how rife these were is debatable. They were not, in my experience, as rife as the popular satires listed in Chapter One make them out to be. But be this as it may, our interest here is not in the past, or with the justice of these complaints, or even with the principle of accountability. Let it be acknowledged that universities can reasonably be asked to justify public expenditure by promoting rich and energetic research work. The question then is: have the new conditions under which they operate brought it about that they do this?

It is difficult to answer this question decisively, but there is some reason to think that the emphasis on productivity and output is in fact counterproductive. If so, however, it is in a specially interesting way, and one which throws a different light on the concept of accountability.

At one time the European Common Agricultural Policy gave rise to very large surpluses, familiarly known as the butter mountain, the wine lake and so on. Arguably, the pressure to publish has given rise a similar phenomenon which we might dub 'the book mountain'. There has been a huge (and still rising) increase in the number of academic books and journals. Interestingly, the explanation of this increase bears a similarity to its agricultural counterparts, namely an artificial gap between producer and consumer. In both cases a system has come about that creates incentives to producers that have little, if anything, to do with the demands of the consumer.

The growth in the number of academic books and periodicals has not come about because of rising demand from scholars and readers, or at least not primarily. It is a result of the relatively independent requirement that academics be 'productive' and the fact that their productivity is measured in 'output', which is to say, published books and essays. The two incentives driving the supply side of this 'productivity' have already been noted, first, research assessment exercises, and second the fact that recognition and promotion within the universities is decided almost entirely on the number of publications an academic can list. Both have been exacerbated by research grant awarding bodies and commercial publishers. The awarding authorities want to see the results of scholarly and scientific inquiry issuing in a tangible form, and in the award of such grants, success promotes success. At the same time publishers are willing to produce tiny runs of books and periodicals since, to make the exercise profitable, it takes only a small number of libraries to subscribe at very high prices.

These conditions ensure that there is a large but hidden subsidy to academic 'output'. Academics are paid, in part, to write books and articles. Consequently, the financial return on the sales of the books themselves is not of any great moment. Any academic who makes money by writing regards this as a very welcome bonus; academics are not *required* to earn money by producing books in response to consumer demand. They are only required to write.

To a degree this is as it should be, of course. Many of the best academic books inevitably have slow sales and a very long shelf life, and many of the great academic presses were set up in recognition of this fact. But as incentives unrelated to demand have grown, the subsidising of authors and publishers has now reached unprecedented levels. The result is that the proportion of the books and articles making up this 'output', which virtually no one has any interest in reading, almost certainly exceeds the number which enter the currency of academic inquiry. As a result they simply reside on library shelves.

There are at least two deleterious effects of this. First, genuine academic book buying has virtually collapsed. Since limited print runs push up prices considerably beyond the rate at which academic salaries have risen, there are few true consumers. Most purchases are made by means of recommendations to libraries. In contrast to individual purchase, it is relatively easy for academics to recommend that their libraries acquire new books and journals (though library budgets too are seriously stretched by the book mountain). However, these recommendations are generally based, not on a direct desire to read the recommended title, but on a more abstract idea of what the library 'ought' to have.

Second, even if most new titles could be, and were, purchased directly by potential readers, only a tiny proportion of what is produced could actually be read. There simply is too much. A strange condition has come about in which academics are writing hard, but reading only a very small proportion of the vast outpouring relevant to their subject. It has been estimated in philosophy, for instance, that *on average*, each journal article attracts about four readers. Since this is an average, it follows that very many articles are read only by editors and those who write them. It is an inevitable consequence of such a condition, that real and substantial contributions to knowledge stand a very high chance of being buried without trace.

This emphasis on the tangible creates an indefensible preference for publication. A published paper can attract as few as four readers. A paper delivered to a conference can reach thirty expert listeners, and moreover, engage in exchange with them. But if it is not published it does not enter the reckoning which RAEs require. There is no rationale to this, in my view.

Since it is no longer enough that a university should have amongst its number scholars expert in a subject, who may or may not publish when they have something of special interest to say, supply hugely exceeds demand. Since anyone seeking advance, or even security, in the profession, must secure a national, or better international 'reputation', and the way to prove that this has been done is to be able to cite large numbers of published works, these works appear irrespective of the value of their publication to potential readers. This is not to say that most of what is published is worthless dross. Some of it may be. The point is rather that the chance of its intellectual value surfacing in such a way as to make a difference to human knowledge and understanding in general is very seriously diminished.

If this is true, the conclusion to be drawn is that present trends have not actually served the interests of public accountability construed in terms of benefits being relative to costs. Money is well spent on the promotion of academic research if the result is that human knowledge and understanding is increased and enriched. The emphasis on 'output' and 'productivity' seems to serve this end because it requires tangible evidence. Influence and enrichment in this context, however, is essentially intangible (which is not to say inestimable), and the language of production, drawn as it is from the relatively alien context of commerce and industry, in fact works against it. The point is not that more means worse, though it may do, but that more means less, paradoxical though this may sound. The more books and papers that are produced, the less they contribute to the real enrichment of knowledge and understanding.

Research Proposals

This leaves us with a question. How *is* intellectual enrichment to be assessed? How are we to know that money spent on intellectual research is money well spent? This is a question that can be raised by a private trust or donor, as much as by the state and the taxpayer. One alternative to RAE would be (in the jargon) to make one of 'minor volume factors' the major criterion of assessment and make far greater use of the system of competitive research proposals. The RAEs purpose is to provide a basis for the distribution of block grants to whole institutions for the continuing support of research in general. How it is distributed within universities is a matter for them. Many have in fact adopted small-scale schemes modelled along the same lines as the system used by the Research Councils (as opposed to the Funding Councils). This system aims to assess the merits of intellectual research not in retrospect and on the basis of work already done, but in prospect, on the basis of research someone proposes to undertake. Under this alternative scheme, individuals and groups of researchers present research proposals which are scrutinised by experts, and sums of money, greatly varying in size, are awarded accordingly — for release from teaching and administrative commitments, the employment of assistants, the purchase of equipment, the cost of expeditions, and so on. Might such a scheme not be adopted in general such that all or almost all support for research took this form?

Its strengths are as follows. Under RAEs the assessment is based on work already done, while the funds it secures are for future research. There is of course no guarantee that future work will reach the same standards as past work, and hence no way of assuring that what is being paid for is in fact worth paying for. Under the system of research proposals, the work paid for is the work done, and past research figures, more intelligibly, act as a guide to future success on the basis of a track record. Second, under this system the money awarded goes to the institutions where the work is done, thus avoiding some of the problems of the 'snapshot' nature of RAEs. Third, since research proposals have to be costed by those who will undertake the research, there is a closer, more easily monitored relation between reasonable cost and actual expenditure.

These strengths, many would argue, are more apparent than real, however. The most that can be judged in advance is the plausibility of the proposal. There is still no guarantee that the money will be well spent, that is, that in return for it there will be genuine intellectual enrichment or advance. Another objection is that reliance on track record inevitably weights the system against newcomers, whereas it is often the case that the best intellectual work is done by younger minds whom block grants more easily support. Third the system is cumbersome and expensive; the cost in terms of the administrative and academic time consumed by writing, processing and assessing research proposals is very great, much greater than a block grant system such as RAEs. But most importantly, as with RAEs, the idea itself is importantly flawed. Even if the monitoring of cost and expenditure is better under a proposals system, this is still far removed from the idea of getting value for money, because the value of the outcome cannot, by the nature of the case, be estimated in these terms. Modern scientific research is expensive and historical research is relatively cheap. But who is to say whether the pursuit of a deeper understanding of the Dead Sea Scrolls is more or less valuable than the pursuit of a deeper understanding of galaxy formation? The very idea of comparing them along these lines makes no sense in fact. Both are worthwhile because both are intellectually substantial issues which take their significance from long-standing traditions of inquiry. That is as far as we can go with the question of their value. Research proposals, it seems, are no better in the abstract or in their implementation than general research assessment.

When, as in this case, the conclusions are all negative, they give rise to an understandable impatience. Don't we need *some* system, however flawed, by which relatively scarce resources can be distributed in a reasonably intelligent and equitable way, albeit one which inevitably falls short, perhaps very far short, of the ideal? The question itself implies the answer 'Yes', and many will find in it sufficient licence to set on one side the conceptual issues with which the last few sections of this chapter have been concerned. What we have, and are likely to go on having, the argument runs, is a mix of RAEs by the Funding Councils and research proposal schemes administered by Research Councils and charitable trusts. The only interest, from a practical point of view, seems to be that these are run with reasonable administrative efficiency and subject to regular cost/benefit review.

While I am myself sympathetic to this retreat to the practical, it reveals, I think, how far the present world of universities has come from an idea of the university which it is the principal purpose of this book to recover. Consider again the question: who is to say whether the pursuit of a deeper understanding of the Dead Sea Scrolls is more or less valuable than the pursuit of a deeper understanding of galaxy formation? One possible answer is — those who are *entrusted* with decisions of this sort. The same point can be made about the distribution of scarce resources. The best way to ensure that money is well spent is to leave the decision to those who have a serious commitment to the values its expenditure is intended to realize and the expertise to adjudicate between them. It is along these lines that Sports Councils, Arts Councils and the like are constituted.

In short one way in which we might seek to ensure that public money on research is well spent is to allocate it through institutions which embody a serious commitment to intellectual values, and whose commitment in this respect is endorsed by the express desire of individuals to study in them and to seek the outcome of their activities. It is important to see that this possibility address the practical as well as the conceptual questions we have been discussing. It is, of course, a solution easily stated in the abstract. So stated it may indeed express an ideal, superior to the alternative mixed system the merits and demerits of which we have been examining. But how realistic is it to seek such an ideal in the modern world? And how are we to know that it is realized in practice? The answer to this second question turns, I believe, on how universities are run, and how people come to study in them. These are the topics of the next two chapters. We will then return to the first — the realism of the ideal — and ask how far something of this sort could be recovered and what recovering it would imply.

Chapter 5

University Management

If what has been said so far is correct we have uncovered good reason for a society to value institutions which are engaged in both university education and the pursuit of research. But how can we ensure that they perform these functions well? Though systems of central review have come into being and remain in place, the last chapter argued that in the face of their defects, an alternative answer to the need for accountability lies in the kind of institutions they are and how they are run. This brings us to the topic of university management.

Collegiality

The etymological root of the word 'college' implies a 'gathering together'. The dictionary defines a college as 'a society of persons joined together for a literary or scientific purpose'. Accordingly, collegiality is a form of governance by which decisions are taken collectively for the benefit of the society's purposes. Broadly speaking, collegiality in this sense marked the government of universities for a long time, which is why their governing bodies were generally made up of 'councils' of 'fellows', that is, bodies comprised of all those directly concerned with promoting their objectives.

Such bodies were invariably headed by presidents, provosts, or principals. It is worth noting that the express function of such people was not to act in an independent executive capacity, but to convene and to chair the collective decision-making body. Of course, every human organization requires, and generates, those who lead and those who follow. Imagination, initiative and decisiveness are characteristics of some human beings and not of others. It is the imaginative and decisive who initiate and so set the pace and determine the course and character of development in all institutions and organizations. Because these are recurrent (if not abiding) features of human nature, there is a danger that favourable allusions to 'collegiality' and nostalgic references to its demise, draw upon a romantic rather than a realistic conception of the past. As a general truth, I am inclined to say, if there is no 'brave new world', equally there were no 'good old days'. Nevertheless, there *are* different understandings of how leadership and control fit into patterns of organization. These different understandings generate important differences in constitution, status and relationship, and some of these difference are reflected in the changed and changing character of university management.

Whatever the past may have been like, the contemporary position of universities, most of which have large operating budgets and considerable numbers of employees, is one in which it is plausible for provosts, principals and vice-chancellors to style themselves 'chief executives' (another borrowing from the world of commerce and industry) and to be concerned not merely with presiding over, but *running* the institutions they head. The difference is not merely one of designation; it signals a striking change in the understanding of their role.

Another important point of contrast between past and present is this. There were always bureaucratic tasks to be undertaken in the life of colleges and universities — the registration of students, the recording of graduation, the provision of accommodation and the keeping of accounts — tasks which fell, as it were, below the immediate concerns of the collegiate body. And so, from the earliest days, universities and colleges employed clerks and bursars, registrars and secretaries — administrators in short — whose business was with these more mundane matters. No doubt there were always some elements of what would nowadays be recognized as management, just as college councils always had their 'politics'. However, it is plausible to claim that the conduct of colleges and universities was generally understood to be divided between these two groups — those who decided the aims and objectives (the academics or fellows) and those who secured the effective means to them (the bursars or administrators). The lines were often blurred, of course, and it seems likely that this general understanding only imperfectly mirrored the reality. For all that, the recent period is marked by the emergence of another class in universities — self-conscious managers.

To understand this change something needs to be said about the *idea* of collegiality. Collegiality is a deeply egalitarian system of government. To be admitted as a fellow or member of a college was to be one amongst equals, charged with equal responsibility and bestowed with equal power for the approving of courses of study, awarding of degrees, maintenance of standards, provision of facilities and use of resources. Though the word is much overused nowadays, the permanent members of a traditional university comprised a *community* of scholars, originally sharing a communal existence as well as a common purpose. Within the ranks of the college there is no division between 'bosses' and 'workers'. The only 'workers' in the picture were the secretaries, cooks, gardeners, cleaners and so on which the college as a whole employed.

It was inevitable, perhaps, that as the life of universities became more complex, partly because of the involvement of the state, but also because of their internal growth, serious problems should arise for the workings of collegiality, but it is striking that the demise of this understanding in the universities of Britain is of very recent date. College councils and university senates were always subject to 'politicking' and the true distribution of power, it seems safe to say, was never as egalitarian as the ideal of collegiality implied. Those who are good at their subjects are not necessarily good at decision making, or manipulating decision-making procedures. Conversely, those whose interest in their subject has faded somewhat may find other sources of stimulation in the intricacies of college life. Both facts made a difference to how university government worked in practice. Nevertheless, despite these natural tendencies and the growing complexity of the institutions, the idea of collegial government remained largely intact, and it is interesting to uncover the causes of its recent demise.

Necessarily this involves a good measure of speculation and surmise, but the following features seem to me specially pertinent. There is first the structural limitation of government by committee and its inability to respond speedily and flexibly to rapidly changed circumstances and moments of crisis. Even the most ardent defender of collegiality would have to admit that in British universities (and elsewhere no doubt) the multiplication of committees reached absurd proportions. Correspondingly, the conduct of their affairs took on a labyrinthine quality in which clear and fixed decisions on matters of policy were hard to arrive at. In relatively tranquil and generally favourable conditions this limitation, though often frustrating to those who must work within it, is not critical. It becomes critical when circumstances are less favourable. When, in the 1980's, British universities were faced with substantial cuts in government finance, universities were required to take major decisions, and the system of committee government militated against decisive action. Its intrinsic cumbersomeness was not its only problem. A committee can only arrive at firm decisions if there is some measure of a common mind. The problem with the 'crisis' of the 1980's was that it dispersed any common mind. It was, in short, divisive, and in these circumstances, the effect of committee government is to produce outcomes based on the lowest common denominator and on political fudge.

Still, this would not of itself explain the emergence of a different conception. At many periods in their chequered history, British universities have faced financial and other crises, and somehow staggered through them without any fundamental revision in the ideas underlying them. What made the difference in this case, in my view, was the dramatically altered social role in which they had been cast and the additional effects this had. Having been educational institutions they became competitive suppliers of education. It is in this alteration that origins of university management lie.

Institutions versus Organizations

Between Oxford and Cambridge, since time beyond memory, there has been a measure of rivalry. This was not true, so far as I can tell, of the ancient Scottish universities, or was not true to any very marked extent, though to some degree they may have vied with each other. But rivalry is not competition. Rivals may do equally well. The success of one does not imply the failure of the other, and rivals may in fact spur each other to greater heights. The mark of competition, by contrast, is that, at some point or other the success of some of those taking part is won at the expense of others. This is most evident in sporting competitions. For one competitor to win, the others must lose. It is also evident in the market place. Markets grow, however, so contestants in a commercial market cannot be conceived of as engaged in what is known as a strictly zero-sum game. The advertising campaigns of two car manufacturers, for example, may increase the total number of cars purchased. Consequently, the competition between two companies may be for market share, rather than absolute volume. Nevertheless market share is in the end a matter of volume, and at some point the more cars one manufacturer sells, the fewer the other succeeds in selling. A manufacturer who succeeds in selling too few, in the extreme case none at all, goes out of business.

Two considerations are forever salient in the world of commerce — keeping pace with consumer demand and minimizing the costs of supply. When consumers no longer want the kind of thing you manufacture, or when the costs of producing it exceed what they are willing to pay, you go out of business, unless subsidies or other distorting factors come into play. This has two further implications, both of which were mentioned in passing in Chapter Three where we considered the idea of student as consumer. The end which an industry serves is independent of those who serve it, and the principal constraint upon them is to find ever more efficient ways of serving it. This is not to deny that there is an important role in manufacture for innovation, design and promotion. The desires of consumers can to some degree be influenced by those who supply them. And of course design and innovation have central parts to play in the process of manufacture.

One way of characterising this relationship between outcome and activity is to say that a manufacturing company is an organization, not an institution. The function of an organization is to supply an end, and the mark of its success is to supply it more extensively by means of greater efficiency. The function of an institution, by contrast, is to fulfil a distinctive purpose, and the mark of its success lies in the manner rather than the degree to which it does this. For example, the institutions of justice — police, courts, prisons — cannot be judged in terms of productivity, despite some recent, absurd attempts to think of them in this way. Policemen who make no arrests, courts which convict no one, and prisons that are empty, are not *necessarily* failures. In fact this might be the mark of their success. In the normal course of things it would be a mark of failure, certainly, but this is because we live in an imperfect world. A world in which there were no crimes, and hence no convictions or prisoners, *could* be one in which the effectiveness of policing and the impeccable justice system forestalled all inclination to criminality. Would-be criminals in such a world would know that they were certain to be caught and certain to be convicted. Conversely, no one who had *not* committed a crime would be convicted, and hence there would be no innocent people in prison either. Notice that in theory the same result — no criminals, no convictions — could be secured by a reign of state terror. The important difference is that in such circumstances while the same result would be achieved, it would have been achieved in the wrong way. But since the outcome in both is the same, the wrongness of the means cannot be characterized in terms of inefficiency.

The crimeless world is a fantasy, one in which we will never live, this side of the grave. But the very fact that it is conceivable is sufficient to illustrate one important conceptual difference between two sorts of social entity, a difference I have labelled with the terms 'organization' and 'institution'. It also serves to illustrate a feature of more likely worlds, that a diminishing number of arrests, convictions and imprisonment can on occasions be regarded as a measure of *success* in the administration of justice. By contrast, it could *never* be a mark of their success that shops had no sales and factories produced nothing. *Organizations* that are largely inactive, or have diminishing levels of activity, are failures. *Institutions* of which this is true may well be succeeding.

It is not difficult to find other examples of social institutions. Although it is the case that most modern legislatures pass more and more legislation, a Parliament might be successful just in so far as it was less productive in this respect, failing to pass most bills into law because it found them to be inappropriate or unnecessary. Arguably, in fact, greater legislative 'productivity' is a sign of failure to govern well.

The administration of justice and the manufacture of cars fall clearly on one side and the other if we differentiate between organizations and institutions in the way I have done. It is not a distinction that is always easy to apply, however. Consider for example the Church. On the one hand, the *manner* in which it conducts its business is everything; there is no (religious) point in winning converts or boosting the numbers of worshippers by means of payment, the promise of political advantage, or social respectability, though all of these have played their part in the Church's history from time to time. On the other hand, an important part of its mission is to 'win souls for Christ' and if no souls are won, or the number is dropping steadily, this has to be cause for concern. Full churches are no guarantee of success — it depends how they came to be full — but empty ones are indeed marks of failure. The Church, it seems, has a dual nature at least with respect to the terms we have been employing. This 'mixed' character is found elsewhere. Take the case of a health service. Does it efficiently make more people well? This is obviously a relevant question. At the same time, its productivity depends upon there being sick people, and this is not something we want to see on the increase. It follows that we cannot operate with a simple notion of productivity. What now of universities? Are they organizations, or institutions, or some mixture of the two?

Administration versus Management

The distinction between organizations and institutions is obviously not exhaustive. Nor is it intended to be, but it helps, I think, to provide a framework within which to think about some important issues in which contemporary universities are embroiled. There is a case to be made for the claim that the mediaeval and early modern universities were, in my sense, institutions not organizations. Their function was to promote certain purposes, not to supply a demand. Their students were not customers and their fellows were not suppliers. This, though plausible, is in my view too simple an account of their position, because they functioned in the wider context of the church and legal system both of which did make extraneous demands upon the universities. However this may be, it is evident that in the twentieth century the position is radically altered. It may be still be wrong, or at least seriously misleading, to think of students as customers (though there is something more to be said about this shortly), but there *is* a customer, namely the government. Central government sees itself, and is seen by the public, as at least in large part the purchaser of a good — higher education — and accordingly universities are seen as more or less efficient suppliers of it. This change has come about because, rightly or wrongly, governments are believed to have the duty to secure a population sufficiently educated to provide the high level of prosperity that any modern economy is expected to achieve, and this includes tertiary no less than primary and secondary education. It is this change in perception that alone makes sense of familiar remarks about providing Britain with the skilled personnel it requires to compete in the world of the twenty-first century. From the 1920's on governments have increasingly been thought of as not merely supporting, but *investing in* universities. The difference is crucial to understanding the change that has come about. Moreover, the return from this investment is believed to depend to a considerable degree on increased participation levels, hence the dramatic expansion in the number of institutions and the numbers of people attending them. The huge scale of this expansion is not always appreciated. As recently as 1945 only two and a half percent of the relevant age group went to university. By 1995 it was well over thirty percent. By 2001, the government approved 'target' had become 50%.

Not surprisingly this has had a number of important consequences. First, universities are now very large institutions responsible for the expenditure of equally large sums of money. Second, with this increase in scale, and its near total dependence on government finance, a much more strenuous attention to public accountability is only to be expected. But third, and most important, universities *are* now competitors and not merely rivals. Competition exists at two levels. Since the resources of the state are not unlimited, there is competition for government finance, albeit one mediated through the Funding and Research Councils, a competition which is itself conditioned by the existence of other major claimants on the public purse. Furthermore, however, and somewhat oddly perhaps, as the level of participation has risen there is competition for students. There are now so many universities so completely dependent on student finance in one way or another, that the flourishing, if not the survival, of almost all depends upon their attracting and retaining students, and this competition is exacerbated by changing population structure. Accordingly, a range of decisions have to be made which did not have to be made before — how to pursue and promote the successful and not merely the worthwhile, how best to distribute a large recurrent, but varying, income, how to manage extensive portfolios of property and equipment, and how to oversee long lists of employees of very varied kinds. In their turn these questions generate a need for marketing, personnel management including hiring and firing, and a conception of corporate responsibility which, if not in itself new, is greatly altered.

One way of putting this is to say that universities have become big business. The limitations on this way of speaking are yet to be explored, but it is easy to see that it has sufficient substance to render the old model of collegial government served by administrators outmoded, and this explains the move from administration to management.

It was for this reason and in this spirit that the Jarrett review of university government was undertaken. Jarrett recommended wider use of 'line' management, modelled in good measure on contemporary business practice, or what was believed to be business practice.

Following its recommendations major changes were set in train. The import of these changes cannot be outlined completely, because, in my view, not enough time has yet elapsed for them to be assessed fully. What they plainly did do, however, was to conflate the hitherto broadly distinct classes of academic and administrator. Whereas formerly university employees could be divided into two almost exclusive classes — those who were academics full time and whose role in running affairs was restricted to meetings, and those who were full time administrators (or other functionaries), charged with carrying out the policies and procedures determined by committees of academics — there now came into being a class of people who were academics by education and background, but who were seconded full time — sometimes for limited periods, sometimes permanently — to manage.

Such academic managers were the pattern in North America long before they came to prominence in Britain. Their emergence has coincided with — perhaps it has caused — an increasing use of the language of business in the conduct of universities. Universities now issue 'mission statements' according to which their role is to 'deliver' education, they engage in 'strategic planning', adopt 'logos' in an attempt to create a 'corporate image', 'market' their 'products' and issue glossy annual reports in the same way that banks, insurance companies or airlines do. It is also true that in the discussion of terms and conditions, and especially rates of pay for academics as well as all the other ranks of employees, principals and vice-chancellors have come to be referred to (though to a lesser degree actually thought of) as 'the employers'. The Association of University Teachers (AUT), unlike the Law Society or the British Medical Association, has become a union, affiliated to the TUC. Even the application and review of academic standards has been affected, as we saw earlier, with the introduction of 'audit'. All these are ways of thinking and speaking which were alien and would have been universally regarded as quite out of place only a very short time ago.

To reach a judicious assessment of the merits and demerits of this change is a difficult matter. Because the language of business is still alien to many of those teaching in universities, it attracts a measure of ridicule and resentment from them. Others, who believe themselves to be more abreast of the radically altered world of the university and who have taken more readily to the new form of management, have adopted the new ways of speaking and thinking with almost slavish enthusiasm. These two responses tend to exhaust the field, and leave little scope for any 'on the one hand this, on the other that' approach. Yet, as I shall argue, it is only this approach that will allow us *both* to take full account of altered circumstances *and* to continue to pursue those purposes which alone can make sense of the university as a distinctively valuable idea.

The Corporate Image

How far is the language of business appropriate to a modern university? It is hard to answer this question dispassionately because the presence of much of it in university reports and proposals seems to owe its appearance to a quite uncritical attitude to its appropriateness, and an indifference to its cumbersome ugliness. Ugly and unhelpful language is found in many places of course — social work and psychiatry are notable examples perhaps — but such critical indifference to its use is unquestionably a fault on the part of academics and educationalists, and properly declared to be so. The truth of this does not mean, however, that the adoption of new ways of speaking and writing is not a genuine indication of a necessary change, and it is the necessity of this change, rather than more superficial questions of style, into which it is most important to inquire.

Certain facts seem to me incontestable. The modern university is large and does require structures and mechanisms for the effective pursuit of its affairs and for the successful management of a great many personnel which older universities did not. Furthermore, it does need to compete for state finance and for students as units of resource. Its success in this is probably assisted by a more professional approach to publicity and public relations than was hitherto the case. There are saleable skills and facilities that can find buyers beyond the world of education strictly conceived — hence the conference, catering and holiday markets in which many universities now engage. These are genuinely business pursuits, whose profits can contribute significantly if not substantially to the central purposes of the university. It is perfectly acceptable, therefore, that they should be run along business lines, and this may require a measure of consequent change in other parts of a university's organization.

However, these facts do nothing to support the much more ambitious contention that universities are themselves businesses. Important social and economic changes have brought it about that much of the style of the modern British university, both of management and presentation, is appropriately modelled on commerce and industry.

To deny that this is so, it seems to me, is indeed to fly in the face of reality, an accusation that can reasonably be levelled at some academic critics of recent developments. The crucial mistake that many of their opponents make, on the other hand, is to think that the spirit of commerce and industry should, or could, enter into the conception of its principal purpose also, that, so to speak, the heart of the university must itself be adapted to the corporate image.

To see that this is a mistake, as it seems to me to be, we have only to rehearse another set of incontestable facts, several of which have been mentioned in previous chapters. Education and research are not valuable solely for the material benefits they may bring; man cannot live by bread alone, or at least it would be a much poorer life in which we wanted or were required to. Educational accomplishment cannot be measured in any straightforwardly quantitative way. It is not a 'product' as some other things are. The value of different educational accomplishments is incommensurable. It makes no sense to try to compare advances in cosmological theory with more subtle literary criticism or improvements in surgical procedures. There is no balance in which the value of a Newton can be set against the value of a Wittgenstein. In education the 'customer' is never king. Students need not only to learn, but to be taught what is worth learning. They are thus not the equal of their teachers, and their teachers, or the institutions in which they work, do not 'serve' the needs or desires of students in any plain meaning of the word. Government policy cannot settle which intellectual avenues are promising and which are not; only intellectuals who are free to engage actively in their subjects can do this. And so on.

Because parallel observations to these cannot be made for manufacturing or insurance, there is solid reason to conclude that, while it is wrong to refuse to adopt it at all, it is also profoundly mistaken to go too far in applying the language and practice of commerce and industry to the conduct of universities. Such a modest conclusion, I imagine, would find few detractors. This is because it leaves unanswered the critical question — how far is too far? — and plausible answers to this question will surely vary from context to context. There is one place however where a general line can be drawn with reasonable clarity, and this relates to the topic of the present chapter — university management.

Workers and Bosses

Whatever steps may be taken to blur it, or to ameliorate the strife it can give rise too, most businesses embody the distinction between bosses and workers. In the Victorian period, in which Marx wrote, the bosses were usually also the owners. An important change between then and now, one that has serious implications for Marxist theory in my opinion, is that the identification of bosses with owners has more or less ended, thanks in large part to the enormous expansion of institutional stock holders. Today, for almost any business of any size (though there are notable exceptions), it is the managers not the owners *per se* who are the bosses, though it is common for senior managers to hold shares in the company they manage. That is to say, it is managers who take all the most important decisions about how the business is run, including the power of hiring and firing, promotion and demotion. They also determine its aims and direction and hence its success or failure. Economists and others have done a lot of interesting work on co-operative enterprise and the social market, but whatever is to be said about the desirability and practicability of these in theory, it is a fact that they form a very small part of contemporary commerce and industry, the organization of which is still structured mainly around this fundamental division.

Modern management is partly a matter of style. It is chiefly this part that the shift from administration to management in universities has copied. A different, more substantial question is this: should university managers also be viewed as bosses? It is worth observing that in answer to it, contemporary realities send mixed signals. Most universities are now headed by 'executives' or 'senior management groups' comprising the principal or vice-chancellor and his (or her) most senior assistants, and these are bodies with great decision making powers. On the other hand there are still Councils, Courts and Senates with some form of representative composition in whom the ultimate authority resides, in theory at least. Although academic tenure was ended by law in the late 1980's and it is now possible for any university management to institute redundancies on grounds of financial exigency alone, in reality those university academics who have permanent contracts enjoy a security of employment very rare in 21st century Britain. The distribution of financial resources within universities takes much more account of income generation than it used to, and there is a substantial measure of devolved financial responsibility and accountability. But 'profit and loss' do not in fact have the immediate or even intermediate effects they would have elsewhere.

One oddity of the present position is that on those rare occasions when academics, frustrated by negotiations over pay and conditions, have taken 'industrial action' it is quite unclear against whom this industrial action is taken, because those represented as being on the other side — the principals and vice-chancellors — are in fact equally members and employees of the same institutions, as well as being eligible, and in many cases actual, members of the union (AUT) which called the strike or work to rule. The important point, I think, is that it is difficult to see just how this oddity might be straightened out.

It reveals in fact something of the truly dual nature of the 'academic manager', especially where, as is still common, the managers are only seconded as managers for a time. Academic managers do not in fact stand in relation to teaching academics as bosses to workers, and it is hard to see how they could. This is because, however much they may control the use of resources, they cannot control production. University managers are not able to determine the value or consequence of a university's 'production' any more than anyone else because of the nature of that production, and as academics themselves, they are committed to the maintenance of an intellectual freedom which works against any such idea of control. The activity and the success of a university depends directly on its academic 'workers' in a way that is not true of commerce and industry, and the role of those who manage its resources, and its personnel for that matter, is not to direct this activity, but to support it.

It is not important that this be shown to be a characteristic peculiar to universities. Almost certainly it is not. But it is a salient difference between universities and manufacturing or service industries. Moreover it sheds a different light on management in universities, which must be more continuous with the older style of administration than innovative differences in style might suggest. Universities nowadays are involved in competition in a way in which they were not formerly, but the application of the language and practice of business is significantly limited by the fact that this competition does not take the form of producing and selling commensurable goods in a single market. Universities can flourish or flounder, but not by better meeting the needs or the desires of the consumer. This is not how it is or could be.

There is no denying, however, that universities have to be paid for, and that in some way or other the opportunities and advantages they offer must match the resources they consume. Here too, but at a different level, there is competition, the competition between universities and other calls upon the public purse, and between the alternative forms of expenditure that the individuals who study in them must forego. To examine the questions this observation raises, however, requires us to move away from issues relating to the internal workings of universities and consider them in a larger social context. In particular it requires us to ask how, in general, universities are to be financed. This is the topic of the next chapter.

CHAPTER 6

Financing the System

Universal Access

One of the four main aims for British universities espoused by the Robbins Report was that they should offer the opportunity for personal development to all those who had the ability to benefit. This was taken to imply that the benefits of university education should not be confined to those who were able to pay for it. Intellectual aptitude, as measured by examination passes required for university entrance, was to be the sole criterion of admission. Thus it was that a generous system of student support came into existence. The local authority in whose area a student resided was obliged to pay his or her tuition fee, though this was largely an administrative matter, since the local authorities reclaimed the cost from central government. Alongside this, students were awarded maintenance grants. These were means tested against the income of the student's parents, but even so a good proportion of students received 'full' grants, that is, grants sufficient to support them through university without additional parental assistance. Before this system of grants was introduced, students, with or without the assistance of their parents, had paid their own way through university. In the older universities bursaries were available and endowments accumulated over time met a considerable part of salary and running costs. Students could also make application to educational trusts and charities of various kinds, of which a great many existed. However, even with the existence of bursaries, scholarships and endowments, a good part of the cost of university education fell on the individual student, and correspondingly a sizeable proportion of the cost of running universities came directly from those who studied in them.

The idea of grants and bursaries that would enable relatively poor students to devote themselves to study is an old one. In the mid-15th century, for instance, the first students to attend St Salvator's College in the University of St Andrews were choristers who received scholarships in return for a duty to sing at masses for the repose of the soul of the founder. Many other scholarships with different provisions were established over the years, as indeed they were at all the ancient universities. The early existence of bursaries is not surprising. It is a fact that serious study is incompatible with regular work, and in a world in which those who do not work cannot live, special provision must be made to enable some to devote themselves to study.

The creation of many new universities following the Robbins report brought into existence a large number of universities which had neither bursaries nor endowments. This meant that the realisation of the ideal of universal access — higher education without financial restriction — required that the state should pay almost all of the cost of tuition, student maintenance, capital expenditure and overheads. One consequent effect was that existing systems of bursaries withered away. It was not that they disappeared so much as that they ceased to make a serious contribution to the cost of education. Since every student could expect free tuition and some measure of assistance with living costs, bursaries no longer played an essential role, with the result that their real value shrank to the sorts of sum more appropriate to academic prizes. Another casualty of state funded study was the expectation that the cost of education would have to be met by parents, or by earnings through part-time and casual employment. This expectation has continued to play an important part in the United States, but in Britain it ceased to figure as a consideration for those contemplating university study.

While the absolute number of students attending universities remained fairly low, this generous system of support was manageable within the public purse. The attempt to reduce state spending in general which was undertaken in the 1980s meant less money for university education along with everything else, but it was not this so much as its subsequent huge expansion which threw the system into financial crisis. The fact that tax revenues are necessarily limited means no government can support a system of funding, whether of health, social security, defence, legal aid or education, which requires virtually unlimited expenditure. It was possible to give wholesale financial support to a highly selective higher education system such as existed in the twenty five years following Robbins.

With the arrival of a mass system of education, this was no longer a possibility. The question, despite the wishful thinking of many academics, is thus not one of how it can be restored, but how it can be replaced, and what restrictions and requirements should be put upon its replacement.

Other systems exist in many parts of the world. These include subsidised loans, a graduate tax, the injection of private capital and competitive allocation of tax revenues. The elements of some of these were always present and have come to greater prominence in Britain also. Each such system has its practical difficulties, their merits have been subject to close scrutiny, and the issues surrounding them are complex. The purpose of this chapter is not to examine these various schemes afresh but to explore some of the background ideas and presuppositions against which their pros and cons are normally measured. Chief among these is the Robbins principle of universal access. A first necessary step in assessing it, however, is to clarify what it means, or more accurately, what it might mean.

At first sight this seems fairly plain. Universal access means that everyone who has the ability to undertake a course of higher education should be able to do so, and should not be prevented from doing so by lack of financial resources. Hidden in this principle, of course, is an uncertainty over what is meant by 'ability'. Universal access does not mean open access. There are university systems that lay down no conditions of entry whatever. Anyone can enrol, and if they pass the examinations and tests required by the courses they take and accumulate the necessary credits, they graduate with a degree or other qualification. With the exception of the Open University, this has rarely been the case in Britain, where almost all universities have, in theory at least, laid down academic requirements for entry. (There is a question of how rigorous these actually were at certain periods in the past, notably in the eighteenth and early nineteenth centuries.) Academic entry requirements can be higher or lower, and have as a matter of fact varied very considerably even between subjects and faculties within the same university. Moreover, in so far as they are measured in terms of school examination passes, there is further scope for variation, because the standards of these examining boards are known to fluctuate. If the academic entry standard is high enough, and perhaps as high as it ought to be, very many school leavers will not qualify. Universal access is thus something of a misnomer. It means universal access within a limited (i.e. non-universal) ability group.

There is a further feature of the Robbins principle to be considered. The supply of financial resources for the purposes of study is not the same as alleviating any financial burden associated with it. In fact, there is always at least one such burden, namely opportunity cost. In a vigorous economy with high employment, anyone who opts out of the labour market in order to study is foregoing potential earnings. Where these are appreciable, the financial burden of study is accordingly large. Opportunity cost is not a consideration that weighs very much with contemporary students, for two reasons. Most think first that the potential earnings they forego are probably limited, and second that the increased earnings potential which higher education will bring will more than compensate for these. This is a calculation that has to be made in each particular case, of course, but it is worth observing that the advent of a mass higher education system, by producing very many more graduates, may diminish the economic advantages of possessing a degree, and that the shortage of young workers (because higher education is the norm) may increase the earning potential of non-students. The point is that the decision to go to university rather than take a job, even with free tuition and some state support for living costs, is *not*, despite the common belief to the contrary, one that can be made irrespective of financial circumstances. Another way of putting this point is to say that someone contemplating university study still has reason to ask (whether or not they actually do so) if it is financially worthwhile. This as we shall see is a point of some consequence.

Universal access, then, is a misleading term, and perhaps, therefore, a somewhat misleading ideal. It does not in fact mean open access to all, and it does not mean that financial considerations are eliminated with respect to higher education. Let us however, for the moment, leave aside questions of what it means, and ask whether there is indeed good reason to regard universal access as an ideal.

Education as a Right

Why should it be thought that university education, or any personal good for that matter, should be cost free for those who benefit from it? One answer is that it is their right. To explore this idea it is useful to consider a less contentious case — criminal justice. Everyone accused of a crime, it is widely accepted, has a right to a fair trial. In reality, a fair trial requires good representation, and good representation costs money. The principle behind legal aid is that the right to a fair trial should not be denied to those who cannot afford good representation. Why not? The answer is that the conviction of the innocent is a violation of a basic right, one which in turn derives from a fundamental principle of natural justice — the innocent ought not to be punished.

To understand the basis of this right we need to see that the administration of justice by the state requires a system of compensation before it can be said to have adequate justification. If all citizens are to be subject to the rule of law, regardless of whether they have or have not given consent to such a rule, and if, consequently, they are to be made to run the risk of false accusations and, worse, false imprisonment, society must compensate for this risk by subsidising the cost of minimising it. That is to say, citizens must not be subject to these risks *and* required to meet the cost of averting them. In short, if justice is to be done, and the rights of the individual in society to be properly protected, the cost of securing justice must be met by the society that imposes it. At the basis of this line of thought is the idea that failure to secure justice for any individual constitutes the violation of a right, and that a price must be paid to prevent such violations, hence the system of legal aid.

Could education be considered a right in the same way? To justify a positive answer we need to be able to say that anyone who fails to obtain a higher education, and who could have benefited from it, has had their rights violated. On the face of it this seems implausible. The first point to be noted — and it is one that is often overlooked in a general atmosphere of welfarism — is this; not all benefits are rights. I can benefit greatly from your friendship, but it does not follow that I have a right to it. Friendship is a gift relationship, not a contractual one. I can buy advice, and having paid my fee, have a right to it. But the advice of a friend is not something I can buy. So the mere fact that higher education works to my benefit is not *in itself* a reason for thinking that I have a right to it.

Of course, some benefits *are* rights, as in the case of a fair trial, which is both a benefit to the accused and their right. But there are important disanalogies between the cases of education and justice. First among these is compulsion. The modern state takes to itself the exclusive administration of justice and forbids its citizens to use force (either their own or that of private agencies hired by them) to secure it. We are not permitted, in the familiar phrase, to take the law into our own hands. It is this element of compulsion that necessitates the principle of compensatory subsidy. Now an argument can be made for thinking that for citizens who are *compelled* to undergo courses of study, a similar principle of compensatory subsidy should apply. Thus, where primary and secondary education are compulsory, as, broadly speaking, they have been in Britain for over one hundred years, it is reasonable that those who are forced to attend educational institutions (or more accurately their parents and guardians) should not be put at a disadvantage by adverse or constricted financial circumstances. Setting out this argument more fully would show grounds, I think, both for the use of tax revenues to meet the cost and for the legal implementation of systems of accountability and control designed to secure a fairly uniform level of provision. Both claims can be derived from the contention that those who are compelled to undergo courses of education should not be unequally, and hence unfairly, penalised by the compulsion. They have right to be treated on a par.

These points are easily illustrated by circumstances prevailing in this country when compulsory schooling was first introduced, and by circumstances in many developing countries today. For the poor in 1870 (the year of Forster's Elementary Education Act) to be required to send their children to schools rather than have them work was a considerable sacrifice to material well-being. For the rich, who generally sent their children to school anyway, it was not. One recompense to the poor was the increased earning potential of educated children, but this was (and is) true only in so far as the education was good enough actually to increase earning potential. Parents who are obliged not only to forego the limited supplementation their children's earnings can make to family income but *also* obliged to pay for an education which does not improve those children's prospects, are multiply disadvantaged. It is thus that the requirements to subsidise education and ensure its quality are generated.

Just what the underlying rationale for compulsory education is is a different question. It could rest either on the advantage to the individual who undergoes it, or on the general social benefit which results from a better educated population, or possibly some combination of the two. All that needs to be noted here, however, is that a system over which individual citizens and families have no choice, is one which, it is plausible to claim, requires the use of tax revenues to redistributive ends, and in which the language of rights has a place. It is also a separate question whether a system of private fee-paying education can coherently exist alongside a compulsory state one, and what, if it does, this implies about the requirements that may legitimately be placed upon those who pay for their own or their children's education directly. But neither of these questions concerns us here.

The position is different when we turn out attention from primary and secondary to tertiary education which, as far as I know, has never been compulsory. If we are free *not* to take part in the system, how could there be a right to have it subsidised when we do? The decision to undertake a course of higher education is like any other choice. Whether it is worth doing requires an estimation of anticipated costs and benefits. Whether the costs, including the opportunity costs, are worth incurring, is no different in principle to the decision whether to buy a better car at the expense of a longer holiday. So it would seem at any rate. To draw this parallel, of course, is to construe higher education as a good like any other. Is there any reason not to do so?

Here it is common, and often thought instructive, to explore yet another parallel — with health care. Paying for health care raises many of the same questions paying for education does. Should all health care be free at the point of delivery? Systems of socialised health care are based upon the idea that it should. What justification is there for this idea?

Illness is incapacitating. If people are to function properly in the normal affairs of life and to compete equally for (and contribute usefully to) the goods and opportunities which social life makes available, they need to be in good health. Accordingly, it is right that the state should ensure what has come to be known as 'a level playing field', both among its citizens and on their behalf. Health, and hence healthcare, are preconditions which need to be supplied if people within society are to be equal.

Such, at any rate, is a familiar line of argument. However, thus broadly expressed, it is too general. Some illnesses are indeed seriously incapacitating, but others much less so, and some not at all. Pneumonia renders its victims incapable of living and working normally. Duodenal ulcers, however unpleasant, are not of the same order. Mild skin irritations do not incapacitate in any significant way. By contrast, adequate care of the dying, which is something we should expect any civilized society to provide for, cannot be explained in 'level playing field' terms.

In real life, even where, as in Britain, there is a National Health Service which provides treatment which is free at the point of delivery, we do not regard heath care as of just one kind. Remedies for minor ailments (bandages, aspirins and so on) are purchasable, and purchased, in the way that other goods and services are, and decisions relating to their purchase are subject to the usual cost/benefit analyses and trade offs that other decisions are. Nor is this just the case for minor matters. Some complex and expensive medical procedures — in vitro fertilization, sex change operations, psychiatric treatment of some neuroses, plastic surgery, for example — are not always available from the public health system, and must also enter the competition which governs the use of an individual's resources. If there is a good argument for health care being made free at the point of delivery, it must be tempered by the overall cost to the public purse, and discriminations must be made between the essential and the inessential.

Without entering into deeper issues of social justice, efficiency and so on, the most that a parallel between health and educational provision will show is that there is a basic level of each which the state has a duty to supply, and the cost of which it can legitimately require the taxpayer to meet. This suggests that while an argument can be made for basic education being a right irrespective of financial circumstances of those who enjoy its benefits, there is less likely to be an argument to this effect for higher education, a conclusion which is re-inforced by introducing yet another set of rights into the discussion — the rights of the taxpayer.

The Rights of the Taxpayer

To those broadly persuaded of the merits of the welfare state on grounds of social justice, the expression 'the rights of the taxpayer' has an unwelcome ring. This is, I think, because of an unspoken assumption that any appeal to the rights of the tax payer ranges the interests of the rich against the interests of the poor. It is assumed, in other words, that the rights of the taxpayer are to be indentified with the interests of the rich, which in turn presupposes that taxpayers are (relatively) rich. There is in this assumption, however, a mistaken perception of the realities of the modern tax system, and the errors in thinking which it leads to are perhaps more easily uncovered when we consider the case of higher education than in some other areas of social expenditure.

The first point to be emphasised is that the burden of increased taxation falls more heavily on those who are liable for less tax than those who are liable for more. This sounds paradoxical, but it is in fact correct, and its accuracy can be easily demonstrated by the use of illustrative figures. If I have an income of £1 million a tax rate of 50% leaves me with £500,000 − a very good income by contemporary standards. If I have an income of £11,000 the same tax rate reduces my income very seriously, pushing me into poverty. Even if we leave aside the impact of indirect taxation, and suppose that a steeply progressive income tax system operates, as it does in most modern economies, so that those on this lower level are only liable, let us say, to 10% tax, the burden on the lower taxpayer is still higher in real terms. This is because, as the law of diminishing marginal utility shows, £1,100 out of an income of £11,000 is a much more substantial loss than £500,000 out of an income of £1m. In terms of spending power, that is in terms of resources available for the purchase of whatever goods and services are needed or desired, people on lower incomes feel the loss of small sums more than those on higher incomes feel the loss of large ones. What this demonstrates is that higher taxes can be, and usually are, a greater burden on the poor than the rich, even when the absolute amounts taken in tax from the rich are many times higher.

The second point to be emphasised is that where taxes are used to subsidise certain activities in preference to others, this means in effect that some people are paying for benefits which others enjoy. The classic case is the subsidising of opera against the non-subsidy of soccer. If tax revenues reduce the cost of an opera ticket from say £60 to £35, those who go to the opera are being subsidised in part by those who do not. If such subsidies are not paid to football teams, soccer fans are paying for the pleasures of opera fans. If we add this to the first point about diminishing marginal utility and assume, reasonably, that the cost of opera tickets is still high enough to make it the recreation of wealthier sections of society, we can see plainly that when tax revenues are used to support opera rather than football, one recreational activity is arbitrarily being preferred over another, and the relatively poor are in fact subsidising the relatively rich.

In itself this does not mean that subsidies to the arts cannot be justified. Nor does it mean that opera and soccer are to be treated on a par as equal forms of entertainment. There may be good reasons to think otherwise. But at a minimum it does mean that a true concern with fairness and equality, and with protecting the interests of the poor, will approach such subsidies with great care and circumspection, because it is clearly possible that they should constitute an indefensible redistribution of wealth from poor to rich, and one for which consequent social goods — the flourishing of the arts — do not adequately compensate. We might all agree that it is important for the cultural inheritance of a society to be preserved, more important perhaps than the preservation of sports and entertainments, and further that only public subsidy can be expected to do this. Even so, there is a point past which the consequent burden on the relatively poor cannot justify doing so.

A similar point can be made about higher education. To use substantial amounts of tax revenue to support it can mean, and in practice often does mean, that the preferences and choices of some are being paid for at the expense of others, and that the relatively rich are being subsidised by the relatively poor. It is certainly true that the financial as well as the intellectual capital of past ages is embodied in many universities, that present generations benefit from the consumption that earlier ages were willing or forced to forego, and that we in our turn must invest in a future that we will not ourselves benefit from directly. Nevertheless, as in all things, balances and trade-offs must be struck. In this case the continued flourishing of universities can justify public expenditure only in so far as it combines *both* the concern with institutional investment *and* a reasonably equitable contemporaneous distribution of its benefits. Those who do not themselves benefit, and whose children and grandchildren are less likely to benefit, cannot be expected to make an equal, still less a greater, contribution to current cost and to future investment.

Serious doubts may thus be raised and sustained about the desirability of 'universal access' funded by the state. But there is yet another consideration to be adduced, and this raises an even more substantial doubt about the justice of systems of higher education financed very largely from the public purse. This is the fact that, though higher education produces general social benefits in the form of skilled personnel — the doctors, lawyers, engineers, food scientists and so on whose existence increases overall social prosperity — it is also true that financial benefits of higher education often accrue directly to the individuals who have received it in the form of higher earnings. The same people, we should add, can also expect to benefit in the form of a more varied and interesting life than they would otherwise have had. In such circumstances, on the worst scenario, the relatively poor are paying for the relatively rich to have a yet more prosperous and a better life. It is against the background of this possibility that we should approach questions of rights and justice as they apply to fees paid directly by students. There are also the

rights of the taxpayer to be taken into account and in the circumstances described these rights are more concerned with protecting
the interests of the poor than the interests of the rich. But before
addressing this question directly, and in order to forestall a certain
sort of criticism, we should first consider the financial support of
higher education in a more social, less individualistic context.

Public Benefit and Public Expenditure

Just as in the case of opera and other arts, the arguments we have
been considering do not show conclusively that a case cannot be
made for public subsidy from tax revenues, so they do not show that
a case cannot be made for the public support of universities. As we
saw in Chapter Two, it is wrong to think of prosperity as exclusively
a matter of generating increased purchasing power. Without goods,
services and other benefits to purchase, those who have increased
purchasing power are not any richer. Accordingly, if it is reasonable
to look to the state to increase disposable income, it is equally reasonable to look to it to encourage and maintain sources of enrichment.
These include cultural enrichment, and it is in this way that we can
lend to the state a proper role in the support and encouragement of
the arts and higher learning. Moreover, we need to remember the
point considered briefly in the last section, that social responsibility
does not begin and end with the present generation. Indeed it is
questionable whether it is even coherent to suppose that it could. We
have duties to those who have lived before us (the sort of duties that
are legally embodied in wills and laws of inheritance) and we have
responsibilities for future generations. Consequently, the fact that
the present generation wants or does not want some social good is *a*
reason, but not a conclusive one, for supporting or withholding support from the good in question. The consumption (or desires) of contemporary citizens is not the only focus of social and political
responsibility.

However, when all such considerations are taken into account,
there is still the practical matter of managing public finance. It is
never possible to meet all the demands that may legitimately be
made upon the public purse. There must be trade-offs between
equally good claims and compromises between competing interests.
Let us agree that higher learning has a legitimate claim to the financial support of the state, that a convincing case can be made for
thinking that tax revenues can properly be used to maintain univer-

sities as well as nursery, primary, secondary and special schools. Any radical claim to the contrary would both be hard to sustain, in my view, and unlikely to carry much credence in present or foreseeable future circumstances. The question then is not whether public money should go to universities, but only how much. This is not a question we can answer with a figure, obviously, for arriving at a sensible figure depends upon complex contingent facts which it is not our business to examine here. The point of posing the question is to reveal the impossibility of one principled answer to it, namely, 'as much as is required for as good a system of university education as possible'.

This is an answer, probably, that could not be sustained for any area of public expenditure. Even systems of defence, irrigation, the water supply, or the protection of the environment, upon which arguably the very continued existence of a society might depend, can always be improved upon, and choices have to be made between these highly important, but competing, functions of government in the face of limited resources. In the case of universities it would be impossible ever to argue, I think, that the continued existence of a society depended upon them. Certainly they can contribute substantially to the prosperity and well-being of a society, and their loss or neglect can be felt in striking ways and across a wide spectrum. Nevertheless it seems plain that important though they generally are, universities cannot claim special privileges, even within the realm of educational expenditure. Their claims must take their place among the many claims that the general cause of education makes upon government support and hence upon the taxpayer. Moreover, education as a whole must take its place alongside the equally good claims of health, social services and law.

With the colossal expansion of the British university system in recent years, the amount of money that is available has necessarily implied a reduction in the quality of provision that is possible, with the result that not only is the system less good than it might be, but it is less good than it was. How are its deficiencies to be remedied? Assuming that the requisite level of state finance will not, because realistically it cannot, be restored, one plain answer seems to be the introduction of fees by which students pay directly, in part, not only for the education they receive, but to support the continued existence and well-being of the institutions from which they receive it. This was the answer, in fact, of the Labour government elected in 1997, under whom a flat rate tuition fee payable 'up front' by students was introduced. In Scotland, following the re-establishment of the Scottish Parliament in 1999, this system was altered so that students pay the tuition fee, not 'up front', but after graduation.

The introduction (or more accurately re-introduction) of student tuition fees led to very considerable opposition and debate, and it is a debate that rumbles on. What objections are there to such a move? This brings us back to the idea of universal access.

Objections to Fees

If we leave aside the morally ambitious claim that university students, if they are sufficiently able, have a *right* to free higher education, a claim we have seen reason to question on the very grounds on which it is often advanced, namely social justice, the principal objection to direct fees seems to be that they present an obstacle to personal betterment, and further, that this obstacle will operate unevenly, and hence unfairly, across different socio-economic groups.

These two points, as it seems to me, need to be answered differently, the first by direct confrontation, the second by greater imagination. Take the first. Why should the fact that direct costs present an obstacle to personal betterment carry the implication that they should be met by someone other than the person whose betterment it is? In almost every other context than health and education, no one thinks this. My life is better if I have personally available means of transport — a car in short. But no one to my knowledge has ever taken this to be a reason for providing cars free of charge to those who use them, and the same applies to music centres, holidays, gymnasiums and a host of other goods. It applies to the most basic goods of all in fact — food and drink.

Even in the case of education our thinking on this matter is highly selective. Countless people pay for music, dancing, driving, elocution or sports lessons. These are all, they calculate, for their betterment, and hence worth paying for. Why should the same connection not hold for lessons in philosophy, accountancy, medicine, agriculture or art history? This is a rhetorical question for the answer to it is plain: there is no reason why they should not. The only qualification to be entered is that the institutions which provide intellectual goods cannot be called into and out of existence at will or in the course of a short period, and hence must rely upon the capital of ages and make provision for the future. There is thus reason to think that *present* beneficiaries of these goods cannot reasonably be expected to meet their *full* cost. But this is a quite different claim to the supposition that they should pay *none* of the costs directly. In support of this hugely ambitious contention we have only the backing of (recent) habit and custom. However, the fact that this is how it has been since Robbins does not show that this is how it ought always to be, regardless of greatly altered circumstances.

Everything turns then on the second objection, that direct fees would result in an unequal distribution of the benefits of higher education across socio-economic classes. Now with respect to this two observations need to be made. First, this is a prediction about likely consequences, and only experience can show what does in fact result. There is an unpleasant tendency on the part of many who discuss these questions to adopt a paternalistic — not to say patrician — attitude to those in the lower socio-economic classes, one which assumes that the calculation they ought to make with respect to the use of their resources (in favour of higher education) is plain and that it is equally plain that left to their own devices they will not make it. We do not know that they will not, and in any case, a true belief in equality would lend considerable importance to leaving them to make their own decisions. If they judge higher education not to be worth its cost, this is a decision that ought to be respected.

But the second point is that genuine response to the needs and aspirations of the relatively poor does not imply the universal rejection of fees. Those who are truly able, and desirous, but unable to meet the cost, can be assisted by bursaries, as they were at almost every period in the past. This is where imagination comes in. The level of fees for those who can reasonably be expected to pay can be set precisely in order to underwrite bursaries for those who cannot. The debate about fees is sometimes dogged by the assumption that what is under discussion is the imposition of full cost fees for all. Such a thing is most unlikely and almost impossible to bring about. What is possible, however, is a highly flexible and varied scheme of fees and bursaries which would make a substantial contribution to the high costs in the contemporary world of good quality higher education.

But would this be desirable as well as possible? Two lines of argument open up. The first responds with another question. Is there really any alternative, except the slow, and perhaps not so slow, erosion of the opportunities universities offer both their students and the intellects they ought to attract? The second draws attention to the positive aspect of fees levied directly by universities, namely a measure of financial autonomy without which academic autonomy means little. This second point relates, in fact, to a larger issue — value for money.

Value for Money

Thinking about how to finance universities, like financing the arts, has been distorted by a certain kind of high-mindedness. Where truth and beauty are concerned it is easy to pull off a rhetorical trick that casts concern with money in a rather Philistine light. Surely, this way of thinking goes, our first concern should be with promoting the best, not the cheapest. It is a line of thought that seems to gather a good deal of support from the (true) perception that educational (and artistic) goods cannot be quantified. Universities trade in intangible values, and cannot therefore be expected to prove themselves in profit and loss accounts. There is here an association of ideas, which, however common, produces confusion rather than enlightenment. It is correct to say that truth, understanding and learning cannot be given numerical values. It does not follow however that their value cannot be assessed, or that the assessment of this value cannot be conducted along the ordinary lines of what is and is not worth spending money on.

On the contrary, such assessment is unavoidable. In the competition between goods and services, individuals have no alternative but to make judgements about how to spend their time and money. Nobody really thinks otherwise. In choosing between an evening at the cinema, the concert hall, or the restaurant, we readily and easily decide in terms of relative cost and limited resources. What could it be that would incapacitate us when it comes to other intangible goods? To make some of them free at the point of consumption simply disguises, and distorts, the fact that we are choosing. It was the belief that this was so which made the Scottish universities at the start of the last century turn down Andrew Carnegie's offer to pay the fees of every student in Scotland. Free higher education, the university authorities argued, would erode its value amongst students, since they would not be compelled to make a choice between it and other goods. What they could have for free they would not value. More importantly in a way, they would not trouble to assess its value, and so higher education would cease to be under the critical scrutiny of those it was intended (at least in part) to serve.

Arguably, the cumbersome machinery of accountability which has grown up in recent years — teaching quality assessment, staff appraisal, course evaluation, academic audit — all of which were discussed in an earlier chapter, are merely indirect and less effective ways of introducing what would more easily be accomplished by students voting with their feet and hence with their fees. To decide whether universities give value for money, which is what all these procedures are intended to do, there is no simpler way than making them in large part (though not exclusively) dependent on convincing potential students that what they have to offer is money well spent. In short, the existence of direct students' fees, across the country, is a simple and effective means of securing the outcome that currently large numbers of bureaucrats are paid to achieve — value for money.

A second assumption at work in much of the discussion surrounding the question of student fees is that universities would thereby be improperly imposed upon by market forces. The truth is, however, that the danger of this, which is not negligible, is unlikely to be greater than the degree to which they have been improperly imposed upon by government bureaucracy. It is a salutary fact that British universities have proved easy targets for state intervention, in part, it has to be said, because of the ready compliance of academics within them. Recent experience should lead us to combine real concern with the independence of universities to pursue their appointed activities according to their lights and judgement, with a reluctance to give preference to reliance on state funding.

This is the other aspect of value for money. How do we determine that money spent on higher education is money well spent? The question requires a two-sided answer. First, though not foremost, those who study in them must be able to satisfy themselves that the resources they could have used to other ends are best used in higher education. There is no simpler power than the power to spend their money elsewhere. Second, and equally important, those who can tell the intellectually superior from the intellectually inferior, must have the resources to pursue the former. There is no guarantee that this will happen when those resources have to be secured from the state, as recent experience confirms. There is then a lot to be welcomed in the introduction of charges which, though they do not eliminate, seriously reduce the power of the middleman, the middleman in this case being government and its quangos.

Unfortunately, the way in which directly payable tuition fees have been introduced militates against, or even eliminates, the advantages that their introduction might have brought. If the payment of fees is to have an impact on the quality of provision through something looking a little like the market place, then universities must be free to charge in accordance with the quality of what they offer, and students pay in accordance with the quality of what they get. In fact, flat rate fees, unalterable by universities, have been set by central government. These bear no relation to the cost of the education provided. Moreover, they are universally the same and thus bear no relation to the quality of what any given university offers. In almost every other walk of life, I can exercise some control by paying for what I hold to be good value, and getting what I pay for. Not so university education in contemporary Britain (and many other European countries). In this case, I pay what central government tells me to pay, irrespective of what I get or what I think worth paying for. And to offset this assault on my autonomy, is the opportunity to fill out indefinitely many student course evaluation forms.

From the point of the student, then, the flat fee system is simply an additional financial burden with no detectable benefits. From the point of view of the universities it is a source of student resentment and bad debts that are expensive and difficult to collect. (The level of debt to universities has risen dramatically since the introduction of fees.) In short, no one on either the supply or the demand side of the university system is better off. A universal fee centrally set is in many ways the worst of all possible worlds. The best that might be hoped is that, the principle having been introduced and hence the taboo against them broken, a better system might yet come about whereby universities are free to recover a significant part of their running costs from those who are free to assess the value to them of what the universities offer. (The question of capital investment seems to me a different issue, and one that I leave aside.)

The government middleman, I shall assert, threatens academic, and more importantly intellectual independence far more than the fee bearing student would do. Suppose this is true. To make it a convincing move in the argument it needs to be shown that academic freedom — intellectual independence — is a central value for anything called a university. To demonstrate this we need, in my view, to recover an idea of the university that has almost been lost. This is the topic of the next, and final, chapter.

CHAPTER 7

Recovering the Idea

In his 1996 Sir Robert Menzies Oration on Higher Education, delivered at the University of Melbourne, Professor Sir Stewart Sutherland (now Lord Sutherland) then Principal of the University of Edinburgh, argues that British universities (and perhaps universities more widely) have been guilty of "a failure to redefine [their] identity in a new diverse world of higher education". Unlike so many critics of the universities, however, he speaks as an insider. "The most essential task" he says 'is to recreate a sense of our own worth by refashioning our understanding of our identity – our understanding of what the word 'university' means". Though his analysis of the contemporary university seems to me both timely and pertinent, the call for redefinition is in some important respects different to the advertized topic of this chapter – the recovery of an idea.

University – Name or Conception?

Sutherland's chief contention, with which there can be little to dispute, is that the changes which British universities have undergone have called into existence a system of mass higher education sharply in contrast to the relatively small scale and much more selective system that prevailed before. The previous condition of British universities was one in which, though there were differences between them, there was also a basic equality – at all levels. Every university could expect to admit students of roughly equal abilities, and hence could apply broadly equal educational standards. All could expect to have in their employment at least a good number of outstanding intellects. All could claim the ability to make provision to the highest level, namely doctoral studies, and all could reasonably profess a commitment to first class research. The emergence of a greatly expanded system put an end to this uniformity. There are wide differences in ability between both students and staff at different universities, and accordingly, as a matter of fact, standards of educational accomplishment vary considerably. The cost of research in many subjects, the ages of different libraries and similar resources, and the naturally limited pool of talent to pursue truly substantial science and scholarship, has rendered impossible an equal distribution of valuable research across the system. For the same reasons, serious questions have arisen about the quality, even possibility, of doctoral programmes in many places.

Comparison with another mass system, that has been in place in the United States for a long time, is instructive. As Sutherland observes: "Whereas in Britain every institution with the right to award degrees has subsumed within that the right to award PhD's, in the USA the proportion with the latter right is about ten per cent." A similar point can be made about research. Very many small, and excellent, US universities and degree awarding colleges are teaching institutions, committed to the highest standards of liberal education, but making no demands on their staff to engage in what we might call 'front-line' research. By contrast, every institution in Britain that goes by the name of 'university' must at least pretend to a vigorous programme of research.

Sutherland rightly says that the differences that exist between universities in the United States exist in Britain also. But they cannot be openly admitted. The myths that all universities are of equal standing, that a chair in one is equal to a chair in another, that a degree from one is of the same standard as a degree from another, are claims which it is impolitic to deny, and hence which are rarely denied. Until some measure of honesty is publicly possible in this matter, the confusion, uncertainty and insecurity which dogs universities and which makes them susceptible to every puff of educational policy will continue. The truth is that the word university does not mean what it did, hence the need for redefinition.

In my view Sutherland is incontestably right in insisting that these dramatic changes must be acknowledged by universities themselves before a proper self-confidence can return. Yet if the arguments and analyses we have explored up to this point have any substance, the ultimate issue cannot be one of the meaning of a word. A natural language will take whatever course it does. It is a living thing, largely unconstrained by self-conscious regulation of the use of words in accordance with conceptual theorising or principled reflection. Those institutions which have been granted the legal title of a university are unlikely to lose it in the foreseeable future, and will go on being called 'universities' even in those cases where there is little prospect of their attaining the kind of education and level of scholarship which will mark others. The most illuminating description of these circumstances is not that the word university has taken on a new meaning, though perhaps it has, but that the name 'university' now applies to institutions that have widely different functions and characters. The crucial task is not to find a common concept to cover them all, but to distinguish in thought between the different ideals each can plausibly aspire to. To exploit the strengths and avoid the weaknesses of such institutions it is essential to understand the range of values and purposes that can give them coherence. History embodies these values, and consequently it is essential to understand the continuity of past with present, as well as to accommodate discontinuities. A relatively narrow *idea* or conception of a university – something like Newman's – figures in this understanding, and it is as much a recovery of this idea that present circumstances require as an appreciation of the variety of institutions which the *label* or name 'university' now covers. This distinction relates directly to the question of worth. An institution cannot have a satisfactory sense of its worth if it has no conception of what its purpose is. But equally no sense of worth will ever be forthcoming if it aspires to an ideal that it cannot attain, or, just as importantly, if it thinks in terms which fall short of what it might justifiably aspire to. This is why the recovery of an idea, and not merely the redefinition of a name, is of critical importance.

The Idea of a University and its Social Role

Sutherland's lecture suggests two other interesting lines of thought. First he notes that it is around calls for the protection of academic autonomy that the friends of universities, both within and without, are most readily rallied. Their concern, almost obsession, with autonomy, has sometimes deflected their defenders from resistance to more pressing challenges, and occasionally, perhaps, has been politically manipulated to this end. Second, universities have been displaced from the centre of political debate. The academics who staff them are no longer, or only rarely, formers of public opinion and more usually subject to opinions and hence policies formed elsewhere. These two facts are in some tension. Academic autonomy, which crucially includes freedom of thought and inquiry, is rendered much less valuable than it might be if the thinking it protects has little or no influence on the general formation of social ideas. If freedom of thought is related only to questions of purely academic or scholarly interest — classical scholarship or the investigations of nuclear physics for instance — it is not, it seems, an issue on which to go to the barricades or even the floor of the House.

This overstates the case. The conflict between intellectual inquiry and public policy need not be very direct. Consider this example, one that has regularly come to public attention. Some psychologists have explored the differences that there are in intelligence and attainment between groups normally described as being of different races. Among the conclusions which have emerged is the claim that Orientals are more intelligent than occidentals and that Negroes come rather lower in the scale of intelligence. Even though these contentions are extremely unlikely to have any influence on public policy, they have been denounced in the wider world and some of the academics who advanced them have been subject to vilification and abuse. Now though I have no idea whether such findings are well founded or not, it seems to me that they represent a good test case for the social role of universities.

Societies can be structured around different kinds of institution. A society could, for instance, include institutions that provide a protected forum in which there is freedom to expound, discuss and explore such unfashionable ideas, or it could not. One that did so need not lend to it any special place in the formation of public policy, as ours does not. In doing so it would signal only that the exploration of ideas freed from contemporary social concerns and fashions was in itself something to be valued. The value of such intellectual exploration would derive not from the usefulness of the ideas which might at any one time arise, but from the belief that the pursuit of inquiry and understanding of a wide range of disparate issues requires freedom, the freedom to come up with the erroneous as well as the well grounded.

In short, a university could be conceived as a place in which the commitment to truth over usefulness is paramount, at least to the extent that freedom of inquiry is regarded as essential and the 'uselessness' of a subject no bar to its pursuit. Notice that this is not the same as saying that universities should act as centres of social criticism. It may be that there is a role for universities to subject the policies of governments and government agencies to critical scrutiny.

But if there is, it is not central but peripheral. The reason to expect universities to be centres and sources of social criticism is not that this is their aim, or even their most desirable function. Often it is destructive, as when students imbued with this ideal take to the streets in rioting. Rather, the criticism of social policies and political parties will inevitably arise in a context where there is a more general commitment to the pursuit of truth and to freedom of inquiry. Universities would not do well, in my view, to proclaim themselves as primarily centres of social and political criticism, not just because this would inevitably attract even more, probably adverse, attention from the State, but because it would imply subscription to the very utilitarianism which universities ought to seek to escape. Critiques of public policy are commendable, but the study of Sanskrit and cosmology do not have much to contribute to them.

But in seeking to escape a crude utilitarianism, there is no need for universities aggressively to assert their indifference to personal and social utility. 'Here's to pure mathematics: may it never be any use to anyone', is said to be a traditional toast at some ancient universities, and it can convey a certain attitude that *despises* the useful. But in fact, if the arguments of preceding chapters are taken seriously, such an attitude is misleading, for it deflects attention from the essential role of universities as sources of enrichment. No small part of this is what might be called their cultural custodianship. Universities as centres of scholarship have a key role to play in maintaining and continuously revitalizing cultural inheritances. Actively studied, it is the disciplines of literature, philosophy, history (including the history of science and technology), theology and languages that prevent cultural heritage from becoming nothing more than the passively observed content of the museum and the art gallery, and they do this by the constant pursuit of new evidence and critically revised interpretation. It is an area in which, as it seems to me, the distinction between research and teaching is at its thinnest. Universities keep cultures alive in large part by supplying the critical minds that engage with them.

In summary one idea of the university is as a place in which pursuit of truth and freedom of inquiry are given special protection, not to the exclusion of useful or socially relevant subjects, but not principally in their service either. Now experience suggests that such an institution is unlikely to emerge, (or if it does, unlikely to survive), in circumstances in which those who pay for it are subject to the opinion of electorates or, more vaguely, popular support. Such paymasters cannot afford to ignore the public reception of ideas, nor can they be expected to. Accordingly, it is likely that those accountable to the public for their custodianship of the public purse will in major or minor ways seek to constrain inquiry in line with what is and is not acceptable to society at large. From this it follows, as it seems, that financial independence is an important precondition of intellectual autonomy. This observation is not a piece of cynicism. Those who pay the piper will, almost invariably, call the tune, and state patronage in bygone eras and in contemporary dictatorships provides plenty of evidence in confirmation of this claim. But more importantly, in a democracy this is what public paymasters *ought* to do; the governments of democratic countries are properly expected to reflect the interests of the public and to be responsive to the taxpayer in the things they promote and spend money on. At the same time, political theorists have long alerted us to the possibility of a 'tyranny of the majority' and it is essential to see that a truly democratic society can jeopardise the rights and freedoms of individuals and hence the social goods that derive from these. It is because of this possibility that the power to levy fees, and hence generate income, independently of political authority, is something to be welcomed by those who wish to preserve and promote institutions of untrammelled inquiry.

The last chapter argued that the direct levying of fees is not contrary to social justice. Properly deployed (which is to say, not in the form of a flat fee centrally fixed and universally applied) fees have the potential to be a useful device by which the conduct of universities may reflect something of the interests and desires of those who study, and at the same time an effective way in which universities may compete for the expenditure of individual incomes. The argument of this chapter adds to these considerations a further, internal, reason for universities to endorse a system in which at least some significant part of university income comes directly in the form of fees that those who wish to study are willing to pay, namely that in this way universities can secure a measure of autonomy from public paymasters who must, inevitably, be concerned with the tides of public, and hence fashionable, opinion.

In short, there is double reason for universities to support a system of direct fees. First it puts them on their mettle to provide educational goods which pass the bar of individual assessments of value, one demonstrably important measure which they ought to aspire to satisfy, and second it provides them with a buffer against the incursions of popular prejudice.

The idea of the university as first and foremost a haven within which the free pursuit of rational inquiry, wherever it may lead, is made secure, is a reasonably ancient one. But it needs to be stressed that it is not the only sort of institution using the name 'university' that can lay claim to worthy credentials. Some educational institutions reasonably restrict themselves to the task of training skilled personnel in practical skills. Others may add to this task the development of useful technology of an advanced kind. Since language will go where it will, both kinds of institution, if they provide chiefly for those past school age, may go by the name of university. But there is the further possibility, that there are other institutions, among which the oldest universities are to be counted, that are marked by two rather different aims — a broad based interest in intellectual study for its own sake and a commitment to provide the resources and context in which this may most fruitfully be pursued.

There is nothing wrong with any of these educational aims. The polytechnic, narrowly understood, has much that is admirable about it. Nor is there any reason why these different purposes cannot be combined in a single institution. Moreover, where they are embodied in distinct institutions, the mere fact that all are called 'universities' need not create special difficulties. Trouble only arises when there is confusion between the aims, and where the structure and purposes suitable to one are forced upon another. Such confusion, however, is precisely what is bedevilling the condition of most British universities at present. Recovering a proper understanding of what a university is for does not necessarily mean reserving the label for just one sort of institution. It means formulating clearly a certain educational ideal and the tradition in which this is embodied. Stewart Sutherland's lecture, with which this chapter began, correctly recognizes the changed world of university education and research. By calling for a re-conceptualization of the idea of a university to accommodate such changes, however, it runs the risk of inducing increased confusion over different educational aims and purposes, a confusion which has, in my view, sapped the confidence of traditional universities in the face of pressures from a largely utilitarian world, and an almost exclusively, and narrowly, utilitarian public purse.

The aim of this essay has been to set out the distinctive character of university education and university research as these have emerged over several centuries, to explain their value and importance, and to display their credentials as genuine modes of social and personal enrichment. The academic in this sense, does not need to justify itself in terms of an indirect (and distorted) 'usefulness' to society. Once this is perceived clearly, the relation of the (traditional) universities to the individuals who study within them, and their role as distinctive institutions within society at large can indeed be reconsidered. But its reconsideration should lead to a reassertion of a role and value that is in danger of being lost, rather than a capitulation to an alien conception of a role and value to be imposed from without. It will also lead to firmer conceptual and critical ground from which such innovations as course evaluation, teaching quality assessment, research assessment, and executive management can be assessed in a clearer and hence more confident way by those who are subject to them.

There is little doubt that universities and those within them must change and adapt their ideas and practices to meet the altered conditions of the world in which they operate. At the same time, if change takes place entirely at the bidding of those voices and forces which demand it, universities become straws which simply bend in the wind. For institutions whose purpose is in large part the inculcation of critical thought and solid learning, this cannot be a satisfactory outcome. It can be prevented, in my view, only in so far as intellectuals undertake serious reflection designed to formulate a solid self-understanding of their purposes. And this means recovering the essential idea of a university.

Further Reading

Carter, J. And Withrington, D. (eds.), *Scottish Universities: Distinctiveness and Diversity*, Edinburgh, John Donald, 1992.

Maskell, D. and Robinson, I., *The New Idea of a University*, London, Haven Books, 2001 (paperback edition: Thorverton, Imprint Academic, 2002).

Newman, J.H., *The Idea of a University* (ed. M.J. Svaglic), Notre Dame, University of Notre Dame Press, 1982.

Phillipson, N. (ed.), *Universities, Socitey and the Future*, Edinburgh, Edinburgh University Press, 1983.

Sutherland, S., *Universities: Crisis of Confidence or Identity*, University of Melbourne, 1996.

SOCIETAS

essays in political and cultural criticism

Vol.1 Gordon Graham, *Universities: The Recovery of an Idea*
Vol.2 Anthony Freeman, *God in Us: A Case for Christian Humanism*
Vol.3 Gordon Graham, *The Case Against the Democratic State*
Vol.4 Graham Allen MP, *The Last Prime Minister*
Vol.5 Tibor R. Machan, *The Liberty Option*

Contemporary public debate has been impoverished by two competing trends. On the one hand the increasing commercialisation of the visual media has meant that in-depth commentary has given way to the ten-second soundbite. On the other hand the explosion of scholarly knowledge has led to such a degree of specialisation that academic discourse has ceased to be comprehensible. As a result writing on politics and culture tends to be either superficial or incomprehensible and the concept of the 'public intellectual' has lost its currency.

This was not always so—especially in the field of politics. The high point of the English political pamphlet was the seventeenth century, when a number of small printer-publishers responded to the political ferment of the age with an outpouring of widely-accessible pamphlets and tracts. Indeed Imprint Academic operates a reprint service under the banner of 'The Rota', offering facsimile editions of works such as *The World's Mistake in Oliver Cromwell* and *Gangræna, or a Catalogue and Discovery of Many of the Errours, Herecies* . . .

In recent years the tradition of the political pamphlet has declined—with most publishers rejecting anything under 100,000 words as uneconomic. The result is that many a good idea has ended up drowning in a sea of verbosity. However the introduction of the digital press makes it possible to re-create a more exciting age of publishing. Imprint Academic is proud to announce *Societas: essays in political and cultural criticism* to fill the lacuna in public debate. The authors are all experts in their own field, either scholarly or professional, but the essays are aimed at a general audience and contain the minimum of academic paraphernalia. Each book should take no more than an evening to read.

The books are available through the retail trade at the price of £8.95/$14.95 each, or on bi-monthly subscription for only £5.00/$8.50. Subscribers may purchase back volumes for only £2.50/$4.25 each. Full details and forthcoming title information from Imprint Academic: **www.imprint-academic.com/societas**

IMPRINT ACADEMIC, PO Box 200, Exeter, EX5 5YX, UK
Tel: (0)1392 841600   Fax: (0)1392 841478   Email: sandra@imprint.co.uk

SOCIETAS

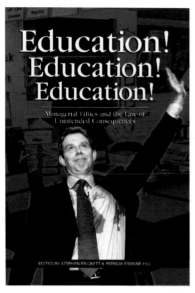
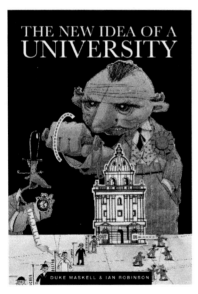